Suggested Al-Anon Preamble to the Twelve Steps

The Al-Anon Family Groups are a fellowship of relatives and friends of alcoholics who share their experience, strength, and hope in order to solve their common problems. We believe alcoholism is a family illness and that changed attitudes can aid recovery.

Al-Anon is not allied with any sect, denomination, political entity, organization, or institution; does not engage in any controversy; neither endorses nor opposes any cause. There are no dues for membership. Al-Anon is self-supporting through its own voluntary contributions.

Al-Anon has but one purpose: to help families of alcoholics. We do this by practicing the Twelve Steps, by welcoming and giving comfort to families of alcoholics, and by giving understanding and encouragement to the alcoholic.

© Al-Anon Family Group Headquarters, Inc. 1998

Library of Congress Catalog Card No. 98-71773
ISBN 0910034-33-8

Publishers Cataloging in Publication
Having had a spiritual awakening...
Includes index
LCCN 98-71773
ISBN 0910034-33-8

1. Alcoholics—Family relationships. 2. Alcoholics-Rehabilitation. 3. Children of Alcoholics. I. Al-Anon Family Group Headquarters, inc.

Approved by
World Service Conference
Al-Anon Family Groups

1-50M-98-10.00   B-25   Printed in USA

Having Had a Spiritual

Awakening...

Al-Anon Family Groups

The Serenity Prayer

God, grant me the serenity
To accept the things I cannot change,
Courage to change the things I can,
And wisdom to know the difference.

Preface

Al-Anon co-founder, Lois W., said: "The word spirituality means so much it is hard to define....I think that spirituality is living a life that has a deeper meaning than the search for daily necessities. If we live spiritually in our daily life, then we find deeper fulfillment for ourselves....Every activity can have a spiritual motive."[1]

The theme of finding a deeper meaning in daily life serves as the thread that connects the fabric of the stories that follow. In many different voices, they describe ways of living that have revealed "a deeper meaning than the search for daily necessities."

[1] *First Steps - Al-Anon... 35 years of beginnings p. 156*

Having Had a Spiritual Awakening...

Contents

Having Had a Spiritual Awakening…

Introduction

The Al-Anon program encourages us to seek the guidance of a Higher Power in whatever way we choose. Though our spiritual awakenings are individual and separate, our experience as Al-Anon members of being guided by a "Power greater than ourselves" is a common one.

We may not always be able to detect the guidance of a Higher Power in our lives, and we may not be able to explain it. We are, after all, beings with limited experience, vision, and understanding. Still, in Al-Anon most of us discover some version of a guidance that, at least from time to time, we can feel operating in our lives. While we may feel it change in shape or focus from day to day, we do see it surfacing again and again. It is this "Power greater than ourselves," working in as many ways as we are open to receive it, that works to restore us to sanity.

The family disease of alcoholism is what brings us together in a program that provides solutions and offers us peace and serenity. While many of our issues are common, it is important for us to recognize our differences as well. "Al-Anon is not allied with any sect or denomination. It is a spiritual program, based on no particular form of religion. Everyone is welcome. Let us not defeat our purpose by entering into discussions concerning specific religious tenets."[1]

This book celebrates the international spirituality of our program. In these pages, each sharing challenges readers to explore their own recovery by considering their personal responses to the question that follows. They may instill spiritual reflection and meditation as well as provide members with new Al-Anon/Alateen meeting topics. May these stories serve as a reminder that the guidance of a Higher Power is the foundation of recovery in Al-Anon.

[1] *Alcoholism the Family Disease*, (P-4)

Chapter 1

A Higher Power Working Through Nature

From Survival to Recovery: Growing Up In An Alcoholic Home contains an account of one Al-Anon member's eventful encounter with the natural world: "With a free mind, I walked recently, for perhaps the first time in my life, accompanied by my Higher Power whom I choose to call God.

"The birds were singing, and I noticed tiny green buds popping out from every seemingly dead tree, and it filled my heart with an inexplicable joy. As I walked slowly, relishing God's handiwork, such awe and love came over me, I cannot adequately describe it."[1]

Nature provides us with sights and sounds that can be soothing, humbling, and awe-inspiring all at once. A wordless encounter with the beauty and power of the natural world can often open the door to spiritual experience.

[1] *From Survival to Recovery: Growing Up In An Alcoholic Home* - pp. 286-287

Connected through Nature's Beauty

I believe that because of Al-Anon I had a spiritual awakening resulting in a desire and ability to love myself and others unconditionally. Being affected by the disease of alcoholism since childhood, I learned survival tactics like controlling, manipulating, and taking care of others. These tactics were efforts to try to get my needs met. Through Al-Anon and the God of my understanding, I came to the realization that as a little girl, I did at times have the desire and ability to love others unconditionally. I got sidetracked by the disease of alcoholism from the beautiful gift God had given me. This is my memory of that gift.

My earliest recollection of the presence of God in my life was after it snowed at night. I would experience feelings of peace, contentment, beauty, and holiness. Even though it was nighttime it would be so bright outside. I felt so connected to God through the beauty that He created; an overpowering love would swell up in me, a great love for other people. I would have such a desire to clean the snow off people's cars but I didn't want them to know I was the one who did it.

Now I realize that what I felt was unconditional love for others, the kind of love that God has for us. I believe that the beauty and peace that surrounded what God created filled me with so much love and joy that I couldn't contain it within myself. That love and joy just had to come out and spill over to others. Those moments as a child were the times that I felt the most loved, the most peaceful, and the most loving to others without expecting anything back from them.

It was a beautiful awakening to me to know that the seed of unconditional love had already been planted in me in childhood; under the right growing conditions of Al-Anon, it is blossoming again. Thank you God and Al-Anon.

United States

Do I see the beauty found in nature?

A Daughter of the Land

My papaw loved to drink. He would sneak outside to the corncrib many times during the day to have a nip. When I was a child, I would go around the hillside to visit him and Mamaw to get away from my little brothers. I always knew my papaw loved to drink. My mamaw would rant and rave about it to the point that he would take me for a walk just to get away from her.

I also knew my papaw was full-blooded Cherokee. He would tell me wonderful stories of his childhood with his mother who lived in the little log cabin at the mouth of the "holler"—at the trailhead of his land and at the trailhead of his life. Consequently, he is at the trailhead of my life.

I learned that spirits of my ancestors are still alive in the hawks and eagles that fly over their lands. Often while walking to the hill above the house, my papaw would point to a red-tailed hawk and tell me, "There's your great-grandmother." He always told me the spirits of our ancestors are now in the hawks and eagles that fly high above us. I love to sit on my backyard swing and watch them soar above our house. I like to think my papaw and great-grandmother have come to visit.

My papaw was always proud of his heritage, even after he had had too many "nips" and began to get angry and started cussing while recounting all the times he had been taunted and even beat up for being a "dirty Indian." I always hated these stories, but I knew from an early age the way that drinking and trouble go hand-in-hand.

I knew my papaw got into these fights not because he was an Indian, but because he had some problem with drinking from those bottles he hid out in the corncrib. Al-Anon has taught me that this is all part of the disease of alcoholism, and when working on having compassion for the alcoholics in my life today, I remember the compassion I felt for my papaw as a child. It helps.

Just as I knew that Papaw had a drinking problem and that there was lots of violence involved with all that, I also knew that his pride in his heritage always showed in the big smile that lit his face when telling me of his mother, my great-grandmother. I know she helped build that little cabin where he was born, and I feel I am a little bit like her—a daughter of the land.

I love to go barefoot, to feel the heart of Mother Earth beneath my feet, keeping me grounded and connected to Her and to the land. When I look up and see "Father Sun, Grandmother Moon, and Sister Stars" that Papaw told me of, I feel connected to them, also. I feel a kinship with the hawks in some innate way.

I know my papaw is at peace, soaring and happy that I am renewing the interest that he sparked in that little girl who loved to walk with him to the meadows he loved so dearly. I am very proud to be his granddaughter, for he was an honorable man most of the time. I know that he suffered from the disease of alcoholism, and I can say I am glad I learned those lessons he taught me about the harmful effects of the disease, so that I can better have the compassion and understanding I have needed in my adult life.

United States

Where in nature have I found evidence of a Higher Power?

Sailing through the Night

Long before I even thought of attending Al-Anon, I had spiritual experiences. Time in the program has simply given me the encouragement to recognize and appreciate them.

One such event happened years ago when I was caught with two friends offshore at night in a small sailboat. We had ventured too far down the coast to get home before sunset and were forced to head back in the dark. True darkness fell just as we sailed into a thick fog and the wind picked up.

Although we started to feel truly frightened, the darkness also allowed us to see clearly that we were sailing in a huge patch of phosphorescent sea that lit up as we cruised through. The hull, the centerboard, the rudder, and even the wake, glowed with a bright and breathtaking magical light. I felt as if we were sailing through the Milky Way and I had such a deep sense of enchantment that I lost all my fear. I really felt as if God were holding us in the palm of His hand.

At a dark time in my life, I had sailed into a place of truly wondrous light. Through the years this memory has sustained me, along with the recollection that soon after the moment of greatest fear, we heard voices from the land.

United States

When has an experience in nature given me reassurance and hope?

A Hidden Presence

A few times in my life I've had the good fortune to snorkel among schools of tropical fish, and I've rarely known such delight. My immersion with them was so complete that I'd even venture to call it a spiritual experience.

I noticed when I floated among these fish that I felt large, healthy doses of emotions, emotions I had lost touch with while struggling with the effects of alcoholism. I felt fascination, excitement, joy, keen interest, exuberance, triumph, simple pleasure, rapt attention, and more—especially gratitude, and even reverence.

I also felt keenly aware of visiting a magical kingdom that was essentially invisible to me when I wasn't in the water. I almost heard a voice saying, "Now you see them, now you don't, but even when you don't see them, they're still there."

Swimming with these fish opened my eyes to a wider world in which I became reacquainted with a sense of wonder I haven't known since childhood.

I noticed a new anticipation about exploring the unknown territory that might lie ahead, both within and beyond myself. Perhaps I could look forward to other voyages of discovery that would bring me the same sense of embracing my experience and my life.

United States

Can I recall experiences of nature that have encouraged me to trust the process of my life more fully?

Walking with My Higher Power

In the beginning of attending Al-Anon meetings I found it important to talk—all about the thinking in my head—and that was a lot! An Al-Anon friend said to me, "That sounds very complicated!" Today I try to remember whenever my life gets complicated, Easy Does It and whatever I am doing, Keep It Simple.

Later on I learned in the meetings to listen to the other members. Really listening meant being open to others, being free of my own attitudes. And that was it—until now. I'm learning that my thoughts are not so important. I know and trust that the Higher Power will do it all right.

I know my Higher Power loves me. I stopped asking, "Who or what is God?" I know my Higher Power is a being but often I don't understand. I find contact with my Higher Power when I am walking by myself outside in nature. I'm aware of walking, I'm listening to whatever is around. Then, when I am looking, I can see what is around and in that moment I feel, I am here, and it is good that I am here—all is well!

Sometimes I call my Higher Power "The Life," and whatever life brings up, I have to find an answer.

Germany

When did I last take a walk with my Higher Power?

Patterns in Nature

I live near one of the migratory routes of the monarch butterflies, and the story of their migration gives me a picture of a Higher Power in action. These fragile creatures make a journey of thousands of miles, but it takes four generations to complete the trip.

No single butterfly ever flies the full route, yet somehow the species continues to pass on the pattern of its migration. If mere butterflies can be part of a pattern that they never fully know, I think the same may be true for me. I take heart in supposing that my life since Al-Anon has patterns in it that may extend beyond my understanding and that may contribute to a greater good than I can know.

While I can't be certain of this, I know it's true for these butterflies.

United States

What natural patterns give me a sense of a Higher Power in action?

Cycle of Growth

I have a plum tree in my backyard and every year it blooms. This year is no exception. Over the past two weeks, it has put out its slightly pinkish blossoms without hesitation or haste.

It has made no demands on me to admire it, but it has also done nothing to avoid my attention. Its brief but spectacular bloom gives me an awe-inspiring demonstration of what I see as a Higher Power. This tree follows a cycle of dormancy and growth that includes an interval of flowering so delicately that it stops me in my tracks. It's an ordinary tree that's rooted in crowded conditions, but it just keeps on growing.

I gaze at its blossoms and feel a sense of peace and acceptance. While the cycles of growth in my life are not as clear as this plum tree's, I feel reassured by the sight of blossoms springing from what I had thought were barren branches.

United States

Can the changing seasons help me see my growth in Al-Anon?

I Hear the Message from the Birds

This morning I had a wonderful spiritual awakening. I became available to my Higher Power and receptive to the messages received. Let me tell you about it.

It is springtime in Australia. The morning sunshine is delightfully warm. I decide to take my breakfast outdoors to soak up the warmth and relax awhile. As I meditate, I feel very peaceful and want to stay calm and serene forever. Then the birds begin to chirp. This is pleasing too, until I listen more intently to the sounds they are making.

Very clearly I hear the message from my Higher Power coming from the birds. "Get inside, get inside," I hear, and slowly I come out of my relaxed state knowing that there is work to be done in the house. I must tidy myself up and look as good as I can. This morning I have an Al-Anon meeting to attend and I don't want to be late.

As I relayed this experience to my friends at the meeting, I relived the closeness I had felt with my Higher Power. I was able to share it, which makes it even more precious.

Yes, God does work in strange ways and through all his creatures, if only we take the time to listen!

Australia

What insight have I received from some of God's other creatures?

The Results of Cultivation

I get a feeling for the working of a Higher Power in my life by observing my house plants. While I don't have a well-developed green thumb, I do notice that my plants respond well to simple cultivation. When I water a tiny seedling that is nestled in good soil and placed in favorable light, I can see the response. If I supply the basic ingredients my plant will do the rest. I can't force growth and I can't turn a daisy into a rose, but I can expect that my plant will respond naturally to care.

I, too, respond naturally to care. As I learn to pay attention to the basic spiritual conditions of my life, I find myself growing in ways that seem as natural and miraculous as the growth in my plants.

United States

What areas of my life have I seen grow from the tools of Al-Anon as the result of simple cultivation?

Healing

When I notice how my body heals itself from minor cuts and scrapes, I get a feeling for the working of a Power greater than myself in my life. With a little soap and water and a bandage, I can prepare a cut on my finger to mend itself. And, of course, I must also have enough confidence in the process to be patient.

My scrapes with alcoholism have left me with more than the equivalent of a few cuts and scratches, but I feel that through Al-Anon I have gained enough confidence in the healing process of a Higher Power to be patient and to look for progress, even when it may seem slow.

United States

Where have I seen the healing from a Higher Power in my life?

The Colors of the Rainbow

In a western window I have a crystal that catches the afternoon sun and breaks it into bits of rainbows that scatter across the room. When I stand off and look at these bright bits from a distance, they look like pleasant but uninteresting spots of white light tinged with an orange edge—but as I move closer they change dramatically. Their spectrum breaks distinctly into a vibrant swatch of the colors of the rainbow. The bands stand out so clearly they seem to hover above the wall like butterflies of light.

I take the experience of approaching these spots of rainbow as a suggestion of the powerful change in perception that I notice when I feel myself drawn closer to the light refracted through my life from a Higher Power. Bright but uninteresting spots become transformed into butterflies of light.

United States

What in nature brings me a feeling of spiritual awakening as described in the Al-Anon Twelfth Step?

A Wordless Welcome

A few years ago I went on a whale-watching expedition with some friends. We set out on a large party boat in an uncertain quest for whales several miles off shore. About the time I began to lose my fear of seasickness, we sighted a humpback whale. The captain informed us rather impassively that he was going to try to move in closer to the whale.

Before we knew it, we discovered that the whale was not only tolerating our presence but he was actually playing with the boat, diving back and forth under its bow, scratching himself on the keel, and even surfacing tail-first. There seemed little doubt he was putting on a show for us. We were all thrilled and awestruck by the performance. It seemed this whale was welcoming us to his ocean and encouraging us to share his delight in it.

When the show was over he surfaced off the stern of the boat and slapped his fluke flat on the water again and again—much as we might wave good-bye to a friend—and then dove out of sight.

I couldn't help feeling that the whale, though wordless, was speaking the language of a Higher Power. It seemed that a "Power greater than ourselves" was reaching out to us in a delighted and playful spirit of love.

United States

Since coming to Al-Anon have I become more aware of messages from a Higher Power?

The Promise of the Sea

A dark fog of denial closed over me at the moment of my birth and continued to get blacker and blacker until the power of love called Al-Anon broke through and lit up my life.

My parents, both adult children of alcoholics, were perfect for each other—Mum began her lifelong love affair with prescription drugs and Dad carried on the lessons learned as a child to be her people-pleasing enabler.

Very early in life I learned that it did not do to show my emotions, to utter my true thoughts, or to trust anyone but myself—while at the same time appearing to do all three.

It was quite a juggling act, but one I became so adept at that I operated on automatic pilot, never realizing anything was wrong with my life until some time into my marriage to an active alcoholic.

Part of our "Happy Families" game was to go to church every Sunday without fail. The appearance of piety was very important in our small seaside community.

"See," it would announce to all, "there is nothing wrong in our family, not like those people down the road whose father gets drunk all the time. Oh, Mother gets sick from time to time, poor dear, but she will rally. Medical science is wonderful, is it not? It provides all those miracle cures she espouses so bravely. Thank God for them."

Invoking God's name was a very convenient way of justifying actions in our family. If He/She was ever real to me, it was as a vengeful force that would "get" me for every real or imagined infraction of the ever-changing rules my mother set down.

Under the warmth of Al-Anon's sunshine I began to examine my motives. Why did I try to get to the beach every time I was feeling bad? Why did my discomfort get worse the further away from the shoreline I got? Why did I feel better after a time communing with the sea—feeling the wind in my face, watching the changing face of the sea, humbly rec-

ognizing its power, exulting in its ability to change?

It seemed a crazy idea when I first realized I had always believed that God lived in the sea. So fanciful and idiotic, in fact, that I ran back into my old habitual pattern of denial and stayed there for years. What if someone found out? Well, what if?

I'm a member of Al-Anon and can choose any Power greater than myself that I feel comfortable believing in, can't I? No one there is going to ridicule me for my beliefs. When I first came to Al-Anon and proclaimed, "I don't believe in God, He has never done anything for me!" They didn't laugh at me then. Why should they start now?

Even so, the God of my understanding was still like the one my parents used, a distant, all-powerful being. I was living with my God the way I lived with everyone and everything else in my life—on the periphery, never wholeheartedly in the center, afraid of rejection or punishment.

We had a conference one day, this God of my understanding and I. "The very air you breathe is My gift to you," He said. "The sight of the sea you so enjoy is My gift to you. The feel of My power is My gift to you. Take them within yourself and use them all the days of your life. Don't ever limit yourself; I have more to give than you can ever use."

Now I don't have to drive frantically from state to state visiting my far-flung family. I can stop to see all the sights along the way, not speeding by as I have been all these years. God comes with me.

My brothers still live in that awful fog, juggling away. Me? I slip back in from time to time, but I don't stay there long before I look to the sunshine again.

Australia

When I take the time to look, what do I see in the world around me?

Chapter 2

Prayer and Meditation

"Every good thought is a prayer."[1] Perhaps then it can also be said that every deep breath is a meditation. Al-Anon is a gentle program, and nowhere is that gentleness more apparent than in its unrestricted interpretation of prayer and meditation. In Al-Anon there is no "right" way to practice prayer and meditation, and—just as importantly— there is no "wrong" way.

There are endless directions in which these practices may lead us. All routes lead to one destination: a deeper experience of the working of a God of our understanding in our lives.

[1] *Alcoholism, The Family Disease* (P-4) p. 33

I Pray for My Group

I learned about Al-Anon by chance and went there because of curiosity. During the last two years, my life was reasonably calm compared with what I have had from my childhood. My father is an alcoholic, even though he does not admit that. Since an early age I learned what it is like to have a drunk father. I can't even describe it. It is a mass of offense, shame, humiliation, contempt, aversion, hate—and at the same time love, because he is my father and I don't have another one.

By God's will, circumstances made him give up drinking for some time. He was in treatment for three years; otherwise he would lose his job. And now for two years our family has lived in peace and calm.

After I came to Al-Anon I started to look at many things with different eyes. It's a pity that I didn't know all that before. My mother and I didn't know that it is not in our power to change him if he himself does not want that. How much effort was spent on minor things, to hide the bottles, to control his money, to avoid fighting?

All our lives were spent on that. We didn't have time for anything else. We tried to control his behavior and control his drinking in every way. When it didn't work, we felt so insulted. Then a fight would take place at home. During the last five years it happened every day.

In Al-Anon I learned that in spite of all that, I should have lived my life and taken care of my problems, not his.

I like the meetings of our group. Due to them I feel some spiritual growth. They help me to come close to God, to accept my life as it is, and not to complain about my fate. My situation is much easier than some other group members' — because my father doesn't drink now, and I am not under stress, as I was for many years.

Now I understand God more deeply and pray more often. I ask God to give all members of our group the strength to live this life without losing our dignity or spending our spirit for nothing. I'll try with my group's help not to make the same mistakes I made before. I am thankful that there is a group in our city that helps people to solve their problems.

Russia

What is my prayer for myself, my family or my group?

Knowing God's Will

When I was considering quitting my job and staying home with the children, I asked everybody I knew for advice. I didn't want to make the decision myself and I didn't want to make the wrong decision. My marriage was still very rocky—my husband was pushing me to make the decision so that he could better control me. But quitting was also something I wanted.

I asked friends and almost everybody I knew in two Al-Anon groups. They said to pray and meditate. Almost everyone recommended that I not quit my job. They said, "you need that security!" I was on the phone asking yet another person's advice while my poor baby played alone. This person told me prayer was asking for God's help and meditation was listening for his answer. She told me to ask for my Higher Power's will.

As I hung up, I had a vision. It was a vision of a giant telephone. God was calling. The only problem was, he was getting a busy signal. God couldn't get through if he wanted — I took the phone, hung it up and played with my baby.

The next week I quit my job. My husband was forced to take complete financial responsibility for the family. It's been five years and I know that quitting was God's will and the right decision for me.

United States

When my Higher Power calls me, is the line open?

I Trust Myself to You

When I came to Al-Anon I heard people talk about a loving Higher Power who was always ready to help us.

I would recite the Serenity Prayer, thinking that was enough for my spiritual growth. As I meditated on the Twelve Steps, I couldn't understand the real and profound essence of Steps Two and Three. I felt very confused. Although I asked my Higher Power to express Himself in some way, to come and help me, I didn't feel a real and intense contact with Him.

Meanwhile, I had been able to think of myself and of my welfare more often, but the situation got worse all the same.

One day when I felt particularly desperate and thought I had hit my bottom, a moment of clarity came. I was able to calm myself down. I realized how powerless I was over this disease of alcoholism and I turned to my Higher Power with boundless faith. I turned to Him because I felt Him near to me, in the same room. I humbly said these words: "Higher Power, help me. Do something, whatever it is that You think is right. I know You want to help me and can. I trust myself to You. Free me from all my suffering."

I trusted and waited for an answer. It sounds incredible, but the answer came after a few minutes. A series of circumstances sent my husband to the hospital in order to detox. After he was checked out he started going to AA, which in the past he had refused to do.

Since then I have never stopped trusting in my Higher Power. I am grateful to Him. I continually ask Him to guide me and to stand by me. My spiritual growth develops day by day, by my attending Al-Anon and trying to practice the program. I feel like a new person.

I do make mistakes and have relapses, but I am also ready to take my Higher Power's hand with humility. I know He is certainly there to help me and to give me the right directions to improve my capabilities.

Italy

When have I felt new found guidance from my prayers?

Keeping It Simple

From time to time I've heard others speak of a fairly reliable method for distinguishing between self-will and God's will. The complicated and demanding plans for my day are the plans driven by self-will. The simple plans—the ones that sketch a few important activities and leave time for flexibility, frailty, and also some fun—are the plans that reflect God's will.

I still may have great difficulty recognizing needless complexity, and I may have equal difficulty accepting the uncertainty of solutions that only give me my very next step. I can have confidence, however, that when I can Keep It Simple I'm walking with the guidance of my Higher Power.

United States

How do Al-Anon principles help me to simplify my day?

Cleaning My Window to God

Once while meditating, I had a conversation with my deceased grandmother who specifically urged me to clean my window to God. While I can't really say where this message came from, I can say that the advice I heard has often helped me put my daily problems and frustrations into perspective and feel a peaceful, loving presence in my life.

When I feel confused, disturbed, or preoccupied, I imagine spending a few minutes on the simple, satisfying task of cleaning my window to God. I know that whatever my current circumstances, the light that shines through this window will help me see my way.

Recalling my grandmother's message is one of my most reliable methods for improving my conscious contact with the God of my understanding.

United States

How has Al-Anon taught me to clear the way for my Higher Power's light?

Al-Anon Changed My Idea of God

Before I knew Al-Anon, I was very disillusioned with so much praying to God to change my life. I would not pray asking. I would pray trying to tell God what to do. I wanted to govern everything and everybody. How horrible! My life changed radically when I joined Al-Anon. I no longer try to tell God what to do; instead I ask Him for direction.

This new way has changed my life. When things get worse (and they often have), I ask God for direction and wait, placing the problem in His hands. I ask for clarity in what I must do. He gives me clear direction. I no longer lose my hope and experience has taught me many times that the problem is often solved without my interference.

My Higher Power is no longer that God who could solve all problems from above and that scares me sometimes. He is much nearer, more of a friend, more of a colleague whom I thank each day after saying the Serenity Prayer. I no longer tell Him what to do. Now I ask for direction and light to see the road that He marks.

Spain

How has my idea of a Higher Power changed since coming to Al-Anon?

Intuition

Somewhere at the edge of my understanding of prayer and meditation is an experience I call intuition. It's a feeling almost like gravity that pulls me toward some things and away from others. While it's easy to trust the wordless impulse that moves me toward activities that just feel right, it's more difficult to trust the unspoken sense that some activities or opportunities are just not for me.

"When in doubt, don't" is an Al-Anon adage that sums up this particular experience for me. My Higher Power sometimes gives me a feeling that I can't put into words and may not be able to defend logically—one that just gives me pause.

Part of the growing spiritual sense I feel in my life is that when this condition of doubt arises, I don't try to reason it away and I don't try to explain it to others.

While my sense of guidance often prompts me to embrace my life more fully, sometimes it suggests that I examine an opportunity and say, "Thanks, but no thanks."

I am always surprised by the miracles that fill my life when I trust that sense of doubt and decide to simply stay open for the experience that feels right for me.

United States

***Do I recognize those times when
my Higher Power has prompted me
to decline to participate?***

I Humbly Asked God To Remove These Defects

Each day I see clearly in my life something very significant: I am not what I thought I was, I am not so insignificant. I thought that if everyone else did not appreciate me, it was because I was worthless. I used to sacrifice myself for everyone else. I thought if I did I would earn their affection and whenever they would reject me I would fall into a depression. How dumb I have been — how blind and deaf! No longer will I sleep in a world of fantasies; now I will try to see things as they are.

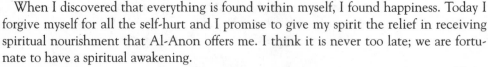

Everything that has made me suffer is because I permitted it. I was hesitant when I needed to practice detachment toward everything surrounding me, such as the way people and things are. I surrendered to my husband and children. I got so used to suffering for them that I forgot about myself. My biggest mistake was to blame everyone for what I had experienced and what had happened.

I humbly asked God to remove these defects of character. He heard my desperate pleas full of faith. Thanks to Him, I have been able to change the horror I had in my mind, my unfounded prejudices, my fears, my resentments and all the years that I surrounded myself with negatives.

When I discovered that everything is found within myself, I found happiness. Today I forgive myself for all the self-hurt and I promise to give my spirit the relief in receiving spiritual nourishment that Al-Anon offers me. I think it is never too late; we are fortunate to have a spiritual awakening.

Mexico

What defects of character have been removed by a Power greater than myself in Al-Anon?

Giving Thanks and Seeking Guidance

I try to start my day with a simple prayer in which I give thanks and ask for guidance. What I give thanks for is often very simple—a good night's sleep, a plan for the day, sunshine, a bird's song. The request for guidance, too, may be of the most general sort rather than help with a particular problem. Still, I feel better able to start my day when I've said this simple prayer.

On the bad days, I find myself asking for guidance first—and on the really bad days, my prayer for guidance is reduced to a loud cry for help. Even on those days, after I've taken up as much time as is needed with my cries for help, I try to find a way to give thanks for something, even if it's just the opportunity to make some progress with a difficult problem.

Throughout the day, I return to this practice of giving thanks and asking for guidance. It only takes a minute to stop and include my Higher Power in my experience of the day.

United States

***What simple ways have I found to include my
Higher Power in my day?***

Finding a Personal Prayer

The concept of a Higher Power has been one of the hardest principles for me to grasp. I did not grow up with this idea but because the people I saw growing most, with the best program, had a strong belief in a Higher Power, I knew I had to work out something that would be meaningful to me.

Certainly the group is a Higher Power to me; in fact, the whole Al-Anon program is, in that it has the power to "restore me to sanity." I heard someone say in a meeting that her guts are her Higher Power. That stuck. The longer I'm around, the more I've followed, "to thine own self be true."

Then I began to think in terms of a power not "higher" than myself (as if I were "lower" or defective), but as a Power greater than myself, almost like a big cozy down comforter surrounding me and warming me.

I've had an increasingly difficult time with the inherent and pervasive references to God in the words and writings in Conference Approved Literature, and particularly in the use of the closing prayer which most meetings seem to use.

So, one day I decided that I needed to write my own Al-Anon prayer, one that fits me and all my needs. This is what came to me:

To the Powers in the Universe Greater than Myself...

Help me to keep an open mind, to be flexible with what life brings so that I may see the opportunities along life's path, to let go and let the unplanned unfold with its untold possibilities for self-realization and growth.

Help me to enjoy each day with a measure of comfort, serenity, and a sense of achievement.

Help me to live with gratitude for what I have, rather than yearning for what I don't have, so that in each day I may find contentment.

Help me to keep the focus on myself, to know that focusing on anything else keeps me in denial and doesn't allow others the same dignity and respect I want myself.

Help me to find the willingness to make amends and to take a personal inventory on a daily basis so that I may live without the burden of resentment and guilt that keeps me from living with joy and serenity.

Help me to understand and accept, as these are the keys to my serenity.

I open myself to a Power greater than myself.

United States

What is my prayer to a Power greater than myself?

Only God Knows What I Need

I want to share with you about my Higher Power, which is God for me. Before coming to Al-Anon, I saw Him as a very bad God. Later I asked myself, "How can God exist, if I suffer so much?" Today I believe He loves me. Having an alcoholic as a husband gave me an opportunity to grow up.

I have found Steps Three and Eleven important to my recovery. I pray to my Higher Power and I give my problems to Him. Only He knows what I need every day. I want to hear God's will and have the power to carry that out. Every day I pray in my Eleventh Step and ask my Higher Power to help me practice the Third Step.

I often think, "Who gave me Al-Anon? Who creates this fellowship so full of love?" This miracle can be created only by God for me and others like me.

Meditation turns me from negative thinking to positive thinking. When I have a problem, instead of worrying myself, I can ask my God, "Help me." I believe He is waiting for my prayers even here and now while I am writing these words. I can meditate about beautiful flowers, friendships, small events of every day. It is good to have a loving Father who doesn't punish me but who loves me without conditions as I am.

Poland

When has prayer and meditation turned my negative thinking into positive thinking?

Experimenting with Prayer

Many years ago I heard an Al-Anon member say that he had been feeling really angry with his Higher Power about the way his life had been turning out and that he had been telling his Higher Power about it. This member's comment gave me a whole new sense of prayer.

I began to entertain the notion that if my Higher Power loves me as I am, I might be able to say anything at all in prayer without fear of losing my connection— and without fear of damaging, scandalizing, offending or overwhelming my Higher Power.

I began to picture myself standing at the edge of a vast, echoing canyon, spreading my arms at sunrise and talking to God about everything—especially my feelings, every one of them, from despair to joy. Since I'm rather subdued, I took special delight in seeing myself raise my voice to communicate the depth of my feelings and I began to picture my Higher Power as a force that could take in whatever I had to give.

Freeing myself to pray with real enthusiasm has given me a fuller sense of conscious contact with my Higher Power.

United States

How has my experience of prayer expanded or matured in Al-Anon?

A Word from a Nonbeliever

The concept of spirituality almost scared me away from Al-Anon in the beginning. As an irreligious, nonbeliever at the time I entered the program, I rejected the very idea of a Higher Power for a long time. "God talk" made me quite uncomfortable. At the closing prayer in meetings I would simply stand quietly, thinking that I had nothing to pray.

Gradually, I softened to the possibility of a spiritual guide. Let's face it, I have softened in a lot of ways in Al-Anon. Then my task was to formulate exactly where I could look for direction. I found that the spiritual notion of being in harmony with the world and all its beings felt right to me. It's really the opposite of banging my head against brick walls—my old way of dealing with whatever was not to my liking.

I have learned to "go with the flow," to blend in with what is around me, and to partake of the beauty of living each moment, whether everything is as I would choose it to be or not.

My prayer times are still silent, I still do not believe in a god, but my thoughts are peaceful, and I hope, in tune with whatever is out there. And finally I have come to see that there is room for spirituality in those of us who are nonbelievers.

United States

Does my concept of spirituality change as I grow in Al-Anon?

Embracing Life

Through prayer and meditation, I have developed a deeper awareness of a loving Higher Power. I have a picture of a Power that knows all of me, accepts my shortcomings, inconsistencies, and failures, but also sees the deeper reality of my spiritual progress — a desire to express compassion and love in daily life. My Higher Power, I believe, knows I am much more than the sum of my failings. As I've heard it put in Al-Anon from time to time, "God doesn't make junk."

Also, as members have expressed it, I now have an awareness that I am not a human being having a spiritual experience. I am a spiritual being having a human experience. I am not a body with a spirit, I am a spirit living in a body.

This reinforced sense of the priority of spirituality in my life has, paradoxically, led me to embrace my human experience more fully. The love I feel flowing from my Higher Power is a love that wants to find expression in the world, that prompts me to feel less afraid, less isolated and to reach out to others. Since my spiritual being has elected this human experience, I feel encouraged to make the most of it by seeking to express the love and caring of my Higher Power in my daily life.

United States

How has my Al-Anon experience with the God of my understanding helped me express love and caring in other areas of my life?

Chapter 3

*The Unexpected
and Spiritual Awakenings*

Life is what happens while we're busy making other plans. Even in Al-Anon, we nurse a strong tendency to bolt from the present to rearrange the past or to plot out the seemingly important events of the next day or month or year. Any moment of our lives, past or future, is often easier to focus on than what we are experiencing here and now.

It has also been said that God works in the present. Guidance, healing, care, and love are all available in abundance, if we can only join our Higher Power in the ever-changing but always-present place known as this moment.

Often it's the unexpected stumbling block or the spontaneous outburst of humor that brings us up short, stops us in our tracks, and spins us around to remind us that no matter where we go, there we are. Always at hand, our Higher Power waits patiently for us to arrive in the present.

I Was Half-Asleep

When I came to Al-Anon I knew that a God existed, but my feelings about God were mixed and confused. I was reared in a home with two religions.

In Al-Anon they mentioned a God of my understanding or a Higher Power. It took me a while to comprehend what the group was trying to tell me: that I have the freedom to make the choice of believing in a personal God.

One morning in the shower, I realized for first time that a Higher Power was answering my prayers. The solutions came to mind and I felt comfortable with the message I was receiving. When this happened more than once, I realized that this was the only time my mind was not full of negative thinking about things happening in my daily life.

The period between five and seven years in the program was very difficult for me. I wanted to continue doing my will. My Higher Power gave me this freedom to continue suffering. I was not grateful. There was sobriety in our home but I wasn't happy.

During this time I became ill and was admitted into the hospital. That's when I surrendered. While half-asleep and dreaming, I could feel a nurse trying to give me the early-morning medication. In my dream my spouse and my four adult children were in a car parked outside. I saw fire all around them and there was nowhere to move. The fire engulfed them. Afterwards, I saw everything really green and clean and my adult children were babies again, running around and playing. The message I interpreted at the time was that my Higher Power was giving me a chance at a new beginning with my family and that I needed to be grateful for my health, One Day at a Time.

I'm fifty-two years old and I feel better than when I was thirty-eight. Al-Anon has given me my life back and for that I'm truly grateful.

My personal God has no figure; it's just something greater than I am that can do for me what I can't do for myself and for the people close to me whom I love.

I try to do Step Three daily and not always the first thing in the morning. There are times I need to do it several times during the day, to make a decision to turn my will and my life over to my Higher Power to guide my thoughts and let them guide my actions.

Step Eleven is for me like, One Day at a Time. Working on me today to feel good with what I do and say is going to make me feel good about my past, because today will be my past tomorrow.

United States

Have dreams provided me with spiritual guidance?

You Still Have a Lot of Life in Front of You

My quest for a Higher Power began at a very young age. It was as if I always felt deep down inside that there had to be more to life than the people who surrounded me. I come from an alcoholic background that goes back many generations. Both of my parents were alcoholics. I loved my father and hated my mother because I blamed the drinking on her attitude.

I felt that somehow, if I were good enough, God would solve these problems. I took on the responsibilities of much of the household and tried to be everything for everyone for many years. I was certain that God had abandoned me because no matter how hard I tried the situation did not improve—until one day my parents found AA.

By that time I was already married, not to an alcoholic, but to a child of alcoholic parents, so my life didn't change very much. The controlling, enabling, guilt, and shame were still there. Still I continued to pray because I still believed there had to be a Higher Power. I asked God for things to change but I didn't listen or pay attention to the messages He sent my way.

After giving thirty-nine years of my life to others—family, children, friends, work, and any organization that came along—I reached my bottom. Suicide seemed like the only answer. The only thing stopping me was the fact that God had given me two beautiful daughters that I knew I couldn't put through that pain. For the first time I started listening. A lovely lady who shared her experience, strength, and hope slowly guided me to the Al-Anon program — my Higher Power was put in my path.

She helped me see that I was the one who had abandoned myself. I finally acknowledged that my life was unmanageable and that I needed help. With the help of the program, I slowly turned my life around. I started listening and asking for guidance to do His will, not mine. The spiritual side of my life, which I had neglected for so long, helped me get closer to reality.

But being stubborn and controlling, I still had to go a bit further. After my husband and I divorced, I got involved with an alcoholic who had a few months of sobriety. I figured I had it made. He had a program, I had a program, so what could possibly go wrong? We became complacent, but I stuck around Al-Anon and grew almost in spite of myself. I got myself a sponsor.

The relationship became a repetition of what I had lived before. I enabled without being aware and took over all the responsibilities. He became very controlling. Again, I felt I was losing my identity. I attempted suicide twice. The second time I was in the hospital, my sister, a faithful Al-Anon member, came to me in a dream and said, "What are you doing? You still have a lot of life in front of you. There are still people who need you to share your experience, strength, and hope." I believe this dream was a spiritual awakening.

Now every day I turn my will over to God and ask for guidance. It comes through people and the Al-Anon program. My world is far from perfect but my appreciation of life has grown. I have found unconditional love in Al-Anon and have been guided back to my Higher Power's path. One Day at a Time, I want to keep working this wonderful program of acceptance and gratitude.

Canada

What unexpected guidance have I received in Al-Anon?

Seeing Events in a New Light

I grew up in a family affected by alcoholism but I didn't notice that my problems arose from my father's drinking. If asked about alcohol in my family, I would have overlooked it and said that my bad situation came from the bad character of my father.

On the rare occasions when my father used to speak with me, he said, "Don't believe that God has created mankind. God is a mere fantasy of mankind. Man has developed from monkeys to human beings." He was a real atheist, and I, of course, believed him. He didn't believe that he was able to stop drinking and he didn't believe that communicating and reasoning things out could help anybody.

When I came to Al-Anon I thought I could work the program without believing in God or a Higher Power. Then one day when driving my car, narrowly avoiding an accident, I thought, "If I had passed this corner only a split second earlier, I probably would be dead now. Why in heaven's name did I pass it at the right moment?

Then during one of those days when I felt totally desperate, I was just lying in bed reciting the Serenity Prayer again and again, just to survive that night. And, heaven knows, I woke up the next morning still alive and a little less desperate. Things had changed a little bit without my intervention and I was able to live one more day.

More and more of those unbelievable "coincidences" happened to me, so that one day I was able to believe that there is a loving God or at least a loving Higher Power who takes care of my life and who sends me my tasks.

Germany

Since my introduction to Al-Anon, what "coincidences" have I noticed that have strengthened my awareness of the presence of a Higher Power?

A Change of Venue

Although I was brought up totally immersed in my church, choir, and youth group, I completely rejected the establishment once I left home in 1960. At last I was free from the dictates of my parents. I once worked out that I had sat through 1,000 sermons and could only remember two! This did not seem very inspiring. Consequently, I developed a very cynical attitude. Basically, I felt that I didn't need anything my church had to offer.

Needless to say, I found the references to spirituality and God at Al-Anon meetings very uncomfortable. Because I was so desperate for help, I just tolerated the uncomfortable parts. I quickly learned to take what I liked, and leave the rest.

After a while, I heard people referring to strange coincidences that indicated to them the presence of a Higher Power. As usual, I politely listened. In my typically suspicious way I simply put such things down to chance.

Fortunately, I kept coming back. I even began to wonder if these strange coincidences were starting to happen to me. I noticed little things that went my way, such as traffic lights when I was in a desperate hurry. I even received an unexpected promotion.

One day I was being given a lift home from London and was in a desperate hurry to get to my Monday meeting. I didn't say anything for a while but quietly calculated that I could get there provided I was dropped off at the meeting place in town and not at my home. As the journey proceeded, I figured that I could make it, so I asked my friend and neighbor if he could drop me off at the church.

Sure enough, the obvious response came back: "I didn't know you were into churches." I thought, "Help! I'm going to get dragged into a conversation that I don't want here."

"Well, I'm not really," I said. "I just go to the odd meeting there, that's all. Anyway, what have you got on this evening?" I was desperately trying to change the subject.

"Oh, nothing" came the reply, followed by a pause. Then he asked, "What sort of meetings are they?" Again I tried to think of ways to deflect the line of inquiry, fearing that I was going to break my wife's anonymity.

"They're just a sort of self-help group, that's all," I said, trying to change tack. "Anyway, this traffic is hopeless, isn't it? I think the best bet is just to scrub the church and head for home."

When he obligingly said, "OK," this time I thought I had succeeded. Then he paused while his mind rewound a bit. "But these meetings—what are they and what do you talk about?"

He won. I went on to explain, as sensitively as I could, what Al-Anon was and how it had helped our family come to terms with my wife's drinking and her eventual leaving.

"Oh," he replied, "I had no idea." A long pause followed as my neighbor thought hard. With a tremble in his voice, he began to describe a desperate and sad story of his life with an actively alcoholic wife, the story that we in Al-Anon know so well. I interrupted him gently.

"Tell you what, you said you had nothing on tonight, so why don't you come to my place and we'll have a chat?" He accepted and I had my Al-Anon meeting after all.

I recounted this tale at my next meeting and still very, very cautiously, mind you, put it forward as a "sign" of a Higher Power who knew I needed a meeting and that my neighbor needed help. An Al-Anon friend who had listened intently to my short story was moved to cut in.

"I don't think that is a sign at all," he said, with eyebrows raised on his slowly shaking head. "I think that is positive proof!"

With that, my quest for a spiritual dimension to my life moved forward one more step.

England

When have my plans been rearranged by what felt like the influence of a Higher Power?

The Humor of Powerlessness

At the end of a difficult week I found myself finally enjoying a brief stroll in the unseasonably warm sunlight when, quite literally out of the blue, a glop of bird dropping splattered on my shoulder.

"That's how bad this week has been," I joked to my wife, "stuff is even falling on me out of the sky." I took a moment to scrape off my shirt, and then we walked on. Feeling as if I had spent the week dodging a hail of brickbats much more substantial than bird droppings, I could only hope that this last little dollop of misfortune might be the sign of a change in my luck. Either that, or the "Powers that be" were commenting on my fashion sense.

I wondered whether this could be a sign of something. Did it matter which shoulder the glop landed on, or which way I was walking, or what I had been thinking or feeling at the time of impact? Interpreting signs can be confusing. How much conscious contact with God can I read into the actions of an anonymous, invisible black bird or sparrow?

Sometimes the spiritual guidance I receive is simply the reminder that I am not in control of the universe and that into every life must fall an occasional ration of something more substantial than rain.

United States

When was the last time I accepted the Al-Anon gift of laughing at my own powerlessness?

A Lesson in Detachment

Some years ago, I attended a lecture by a spiritual figure I admire. Just before the lecture began, a woman in the aisle several seats to my left twisted her ankle. I felt concern but then noticed that several capable people involved in directing the event had gathered around her. She was in good hands.

In short, any action I could have taken to help would have disrupted my seatmates and intruded on the attention of a team that appeared to be both cooperative and skilled. My task, if I had one, was simply to wish the woman well and do what I had come to do, which was to listen to the lecture.

The woman to my right, however, had drawn a different conclusion. She squirmed uncomfortably in her seat and seemed unable to let go of her concern. She didn't seem able to let the crisis proceed without her.

I did feel sympathetic to her as well, but I didn't feel able to listen to the lecture and attempt to calm her down at the same time. I decided to detach from her concern, too, and just pay attention to the speaker who was now leading an introductory meditation.

I felt a Power greater than myself urging me to accept the spiritual experience I had come in search of—by letting go.

United States

How has a Higher Power guided me in learning the Al-Anon principle of detachment?

Tricked into Letting Go

My Higher Power seems to have a sense of humor. Recently I found myself fretting over a family matter about which I was definitely preoccupied, if not positively obsessed, when the phone rang. It was a friend relaying a request to bring an odd party favor to a party in a few days.

In a flash, I snapped out of my obsession with my family problem—a situation I seemed determined to worry about for the rest of the evening at least—and focused all my energy on this odd request. What did it mean? What other tricks might the hostess have up her sleeve? My critical response flowed on and on in a brilliant and energetic outburst of overreaction until I realized with a start that I had completely forgotten my first problem.

My Higher Power had tricked me into letting go. While I felt a little foolish, I was happy, relieved, and grateful.

United States

When have Al-Anon principles guided me into letting go?

One of the Most Spiritual Experiences of My Life

I would like to share one of the most spiritual experiences of my life—and believe me, I have had many. My husband and I were very privileged to attend the side-by-side AA/Al-Anon Conventions in Seattle, in July of 1990.

I had been a member of Al-Anon for some time when my sisters and I discovered our dear mother had become an alcoholic at the age of seventy-nine years. Alcoholism, as I know, does not show any respect for anyone, whatever their lifestyle, who they are, or what age. Our mother died when she was 89 years old with two-and-a-half years sobriety behind her. God bless her.

I was sharing at the convention. It was a wonderful experience — sharing about my mother, who had just died in April 1990. I was feeling quite choked up but proud to be my mother's daughter. At that moment, I was unaware that my nephew from Canada had just walked into his first Al-Anon meeting because of my brother's alcoholism. That alone was a spiritual experience.

After the meeting closed, the members formed queues in lines of four to thank the four speakers. Anyway, I was eventually facing the last lady in my queue. We shook hands and she told me she could identify with me and how she would like to meet my husband. A few moments later my husband came to meet me so they both met. The lady asked if I would write to her when I got back to England. I said, "With pleasure." She handed me a piece of paper with her name and address on it; I folded it and placed it in my purse. We said, "Cheerio."

After the opening convention dance the coach took my husband and me back to our hotel. It was very late. I felt very happy, feeling my mother close to me. We got ready for bed and I decided to empty my purse and take all the little keepsakes that had been given to me and place them in my case. I opened the piece of paper my friend had given me and her name was the same as my mother's and also my maiden name. I felt someone had walked on my grave. My darling mother was telling me she was at peace at last with her Higher Power. My friend could have gone to any queue, but she was guided to me. My mother was at peace. My mother knew I was in Al-Anon but never understood. She eventually accepted my change of attitude and the fact that my enabling had to stop.

When I arrived back in England, the first thing I did was write and tell my friend of the experience. She wrote back straight away and told me she cried, and asked my permission to take my letter to her group and share our experience. We are Al-Anon best-of-pals and keep very much in touch. My friend was guided to my queue by our Higher Power.

England

Do I recognize inexplicable events as the work of my Higher Power?

It Was Just There

I always asked myself what was meant by "a spiritual awakening." I was so curious but nobody in Al-Anon could tell me about it. And then one day it happened in my life; my spiritual awakening was there! I don't know where it came from and I don't know how it came. It was just there!

I felt that everything in my life was right; my past was right and my present was right. Most important for me was that my feelings were right—that anything I felt or will ever feel is right, only because they are my feelings.

The other thing was that there is nobody who can tell me what to do or not to do. I have to decide on my own and rely on myself. I can ask people for suggestions and look for support, but at the very last, I am the person who decides what's going on in my life and who must take responsibility for it.

From that day on I woke up every morning thinking, "Well, I am responsible" — and I felt so worried about that. I felt overwhelmed by having to choose among a million possibilities. Any way I choose, my Higher Power is choosing for and with me. I began asking myself, "What do I want?" and "What is good for me?" In contact with my Higher Power my ability to make choices works.

Germany

What unexpected blessings have I received in Al-Anon?

A Lesson in Patience

Driving to meet a friend, my wife and I ran into several unexpected delays. After the third or fourth frustrating episode of dealing with drivers who appeared lost, gripped by indecision or simply stalled, my wife said, rather philosophically, "I guess God wants us to slow down or to start leaving a few minutes earlier."

"Maybe both," I replied, suddenly relieved. The road before me, which had seemed an obstacle course filled with uncooperative bumblers, now became a simple lesson in patience from an inventive Higher Power.

We slowed down—and arrived on time.

United States

When have I recognized my Higher Power guiding my Al-Anon recovery?

My Biggest Lesson

Through the Al-Anon program I had developed a personal relationship with the God of my understanding, and I was working on my Seventh Step with Him. Due to my life history, I felt that honesty had to be one of the first character traits I needed to work on, so each day I earnestly asked Him to help me become an honest person. I realized this was not going to be easy.

My biggest lesson came soon after I returned home from four months of traveling. I am in the habit of taking an hour's brisk walk every morning, when I have my peaceful time with my Higher Power. During one of these walks, as I turned around a corner near a beautiful lake I pass every day, lo and behold, my eyes spotted a box full of jewels. I was astounded. I couldn't just leave them there. I happened to have a plastic bag in my pocket, so I gathered them all into this bag and took them home.

It hadn't entered my mind to keep any of them. I just wanted to get them back to their owner, but I did have a look at them while I waited for the police to collect them. There were two lovely bracelets and a beautiful gold pendant with an opal in the middle. I fell in love with that one! It had inscribed on the back PHIL 4 6/7 21 OCT 79, so my assumption was that it belonged to a person by the name of Phil.

When the police arrived they told me that they would hold the jewels for three months. If the owner didn't come forward, then legally I could claim them. As it came to be, they weren't claimed, and on the thirteenth of December I became the proud owner of all these jewels.

Four months went by. Once again I was down near the same lake, only this time the lake was not so beautiful. We had had a long spell of no rain and the lake was an awesome sight, almost dried out. As I was sitting talking to the God of my understanding, a lady (whom I had never met or seen before, though I have been walking that route for years) came up behind me with her dog. As I turned, I commented on the sight of the lake.

We got chatting, and during our conversation the dog got very restless and agitated. We both moved to investigate but we couldn't see anything. While doing that I commented on how alert dogs can be and said that I had two dogs myself and loved them. She then answered, "I am thinking of getting another one because in the area I live in there have been a lot of break-ins. In fact, I was broken into a little while back, but all I had taken was my jewelry box with all my jewels in it."

I stopped dead in my tracks. I couldn't believe what I was hearing; this was seven months down the track. I had gotten quite accustomed to having these lovely jewels.

Being very careful of what I said, I asked her if she knew anyone by the name of PHIL (the name on the gold pendant), to which she answered a distinct, "No." I said nothing else and was a little relieved in a way that the jewels were still mine.

I then asked her whether she had anything valuable amongst them. "Yes," she answered and went on to describe a twenty-four carat gold pendant with an opal in the middle. I asked her again about PHIL and she again answered, "No," but I just couldn't leave it there. I asked her what the jewelry box looked like, and when she described it I knew beyond any doubt that it was her jewels I had found.

When I told her, she was ecstatic. I was, too, in a way—but I must not lie now; I was a bit sad that I had to part with all those jewels. Every bit of the process was worth it, though; the happiness on her face when I told her, I will never forget.

Anyway, when all that excitement was over, I asked her who was the PHIL inscribed on the back of her pendant. She answered that it was a baptism present to her and the inscription was a phrase from the Bible—Philippians, Chapter 4 (verses 6-7). When I asked her what that said, she wrote it down for me. The verses say not to worry about anything, but to tell God your needs in prayer and the peace of God will keep constant guard over you.

On reading that I realized that it was exactly what I had been doing for some time now, only I never read the Bible because I can't understand it.

In saying all of this that happened, the most amazing thing is yet to come. I said to the lady, "You won't believe this, but if I hadn't found your jewels, you would now be standing right on top of them." She was in the exact spot I found them, which was nowhere near where she lives and not even where we originally met because we had moved when the dogs stirred.

Even though I had had previous experiences beyond

human understanding, this was my spiritual awakening. I realized that there was definitely someone taking care of me and helping me. He certainly answered my prayers. I am so proud to say that at last I had mastered my problem with honesty.

God put me in a spot where if I chose to say nothing and walk away, the lady would never have known. Had it been a few weeks back I would have been wearing her mother's watch but it had stopped working. In other words, I had a choice, but it never entered my mind to do that, and I am so grateful to say that.

As I said before, I had never met the lady before during my walk and have never since, and it is now eighteen months since our meeting. Isn't it incredible how the Higher Power works for us if we give Him a chance? That is all He asks of us.

Australia

What has been my biggest lesson in Al-Anon, so far?

A New Prayer

In the newspaper this morning I read this prayer, quoted from the window of a local pet shop: "Dear God, please help me be the person my dog thinks I am."

This has been my prayer for the day, and it has kept me smiling. With my dog, I am very much the person I want to be, and when I am not, my dog doesn't seem to hold it against me.

This joking prayer has helped me take myself less seriously and be more honest about my own behavior, and just for today it has helped me feel the presence of a Higher Power.

Laughter may not have made me a better person today but it has made me better company for my dog.

United States

How have Al-Anon principles helped me share humor with my Higher Power?

New Insight

My tendency in life has been to distrust my own experience. If not the root cause, extended contact with alcoholism is certainly a major contributing factor. Nowhere is this distrust more ingrained than in my attitude toward spiritual experience. I automatically overlooked or explained away any event in my life that might have prompted me to see the working of a Power greater than myself.

In Al-Anon I have gradually come to accept a less defensive view, one in which I see the effects of unforeseen guidance popping up through the course of my life.

For example, one day after some years in the program I had an illuminating realization about my work. I noticed that the abilities that I used in my current job, which I love, were all skills that I had developed along the way at jobs that I didn't particularly like.

Somehow my opinion of my history of employment changed in an instant. Where I had felt that my work history had been spotty, haphazard, and misguided, I now saw a unique progression that had given me a range of skills, insight, and experience that allowed me to do the work that I loved. In events that had seemed random, I now saw a special, fulfilling pattern. While it took me years to see, I finally noticed that a Higher Power had been at work directing my experience.

United States

***Where have I seen unexpected evidence of a Higher Power
in my life's story?***

Taking a Break

Some days when I'm able, I take an afternoon nap. Before Al-Anon I thought of napping as a modest but shameful character defect, but now I tend to welcome it as a spontaneous and harmless practice that lends an unforeseen touch of spiritual experience to my day.

I think of the slogans that fit so well into what a friend calls nap therapy: Keep It Simple, Easy Does It, How Important Is It, Let Go and Let God, First Things First. I have heard it said in Al-Anon that I can restart my day at any time. What better way to clear my mind and open up to guidance beyond myself than to lie down, close my eyes, and invite my mind and body to take a break? What better way to start my day again than actually to start it again?

In napping, I give up trying to force solutions for a brief spell and I invite myself to take pleasure in other things: the song of a sparrow, the whisper of the breeze, the busy stirring of the world around me. Perhaps I notice my breathing or feel my body relax. When I awake, I see a world that has done without my hustle and bustle for a few minutes, a world closer to my dreams.

With my spirit refreshed, I'm better able to open my eyes in a new light and ask my Higher Power, "Now that I've let it all go, what part of my life do I most want to pick up again?"

United States

Have I learned how to take a break in order to restore my spirit?

At the Beach

After years in Al-Anon, I now have the ability to stop obsessing on my program and occasionally just enjoy myself. Pleasure, too, can be a spiritual experience, especially for those of us who have not known much of it. Sometimes being restored to sanity by a Power greater than myself means simply accepting moments of spontaneous pleasure that remind me to give thanks for the gift of life. One particular incident stands out in my memory.

At the beach one day, I happened on a man selling snow cones. It was a warm afternoon but this is not a warm climate. I couldn't have been more surprised if I had seen a mermaid.

I asked for a cone and watched in fascination as the man painstakingly pried a chunk of ice out of a cooler, shaved it with an antiquated contraption, and doused it with a bright blue syrup.

I've never seen this vendor again but his memory fills me with a delicious sense of wonder. Where did he come from? I think of that snow cone as a gift from a laughing God.

United States

When have I found spirituality in a simple experience?

Chapter 4

Inspiration through the Arts

"Today I make a sincere effort to roll in the clover, kick up my heels, and celebrate being alive. It is one way in which I touch my God." So reads a passage from *Courage to Change* that continues: "Let me make this day a celebration of the spirit. There is a part of me that retains a childlike sense of curiosity, wonder, enthusiasm, and delight. I may have lost touch with it, but I know it still exists. I will set my problems to the side for a little while and appreciate what it means to be vitally alive." [1]

One of the ways in which members find they may touch their God, or make their day a celebration of the spirit, or appreciate what it means to be vitally alive, is through the arts. With their participation as part of the audience or as artists, members come to notice that—just as every good thought may be a prayer and every deep breath a meditation—any act they undertake with care may be seen as artful practice. An experience of the tapestry of imagination that enfolds us all can help us to notice the presence of "a Power greater than ourselves" and to celebrate that Power.

[1] *Courage to Change - One Day at a Time in Al-Anon II*, p. 325

Art As Spiritual Expression

As I came to believe a Higher Power was restoring me to sanity, I knelt each morning to turn my life and my will over to God. I began to express this knowledge and power in poetry and art work. I am a folk artist now. I feel God's love and power within me as light, airiness, and sparkle—and I feel that love and power around me in others who cross my path.

A very close friend redirected my thinking from seeing life's events as "tragic" to viewing these same events as "part of the journey." This was God coming to me through another person. In the past I became immobilized in the midst of fear. Now, Steps Three and Eleven empower me to "change the things I can."

The serenity I sometimes feel is part of the harmony resulting from knowing God as a partner and others in my life as companions whom I can keep or let go.

This freedom is what I feel and what I have heard so many others in our fellowship describe and live.

United States

Do I suspect that I have God-given talents that I could put to better use?

At the Movies

From time to time I see a movie with a story of great courage or caring or love that moves me to tears. Whether the stories are real or fictional, I feel the same prompting from a Higher Power in my response. I find myself reacting to those moments when characters find themselves moving beyond the limits of their understanding and depending for their guidance on faith, often without the support of those around them.

Somehow when I see the stories of the surprising outcomes that result from these situations, I can reflect on my own life. I recall the various miraculous events that have taken me beyond the person I used to be and have given me a stronger sense of being guided by the influence of a Higher Power.

These stories remind me of the deeper, and sometimes overlooked, spiritual foundation of my daily experience. I am prompted to recall that, when I truly turn my will and my life over to the care of a Power greater than myself, miracles can—and do—happen.

United States

In what ways have I found Al-Anon's spiritual
principles work in my daily life?

Music

Now and then I find myself transfixed by a particular piece of music. For reasons that I can't explain, I'll find a few minutes of melody or harmony or rhythm or song that move me to dance or cry or sing or smile. Happily, I never feel much need to explain the experience or even share it with others because it feels complete.

To me it feels like a moment when a Higher Power is speaking to me. What I discover in my response is a depth of feeling that surprises me—not because it's so unusual but because it reminds me of an inner world that underlies my everyday experience. It's the world in which a Power greater than myself supports and informs everything that I do, although I am often unaware of it.

Now and then a piece of music brings me back to the part of myself that holds an awareness of a Higher Power and those interludes startle me with the reminder of the depth, beauty, and resilience of that Power. In these experiences I find an unexpected and very welcome improvement in my conscious contact with the God of my understanding.

United States

How has Al-Anon helped me find a connection to a Higher Power in unlikely sources?

A Song in My Heart

After coming to Al-Anon and participating in meetings and service for a few years, I began joining other group activities I had previously lacked the courage to try. Most memorably, I attended a sing-along concert at which the audience of several thousand also served as the chorus.

For a few hours I became part of a large, festive group of strangers who had joined together, literally, to give voice to a joyful noise. I was astonished to hear the music we could make when we all sang in harmony.

I felt a spirit of celebration, generosity, and cooperation that I shall never forget. Most moving of all, after the concert had ended and we began to exit, the singing continued. I felt encouraged, if not actually to step out singing into the street, at least to keep a song in my heart. In this joyful persistence of song I felt a great spirit flow into the street and guide my steps home.

Finding my voice in Al-Anon, so to speak, had allowed me to actually join the chorus and lift my voice in song. That enthusiastic amateur chorus had served for several hours as a Power greater than myself working to restore me to sanity.

United States

Have I learned to work in harmony with others?

Accepting My Mistakes

A few years ago at a quilt exhibition I saw a quilt that, in addition to being striking, had a spiritual lesson for me in the writing accompanying it. All such quilts, it seems, include a deliberate mistake in their design as a reminder to all who make, use, or even view, them that only God is perfect.

In addition to the humility and faith manifested in this choice, I also take heart from the notion that, after long and painstaking practice, I may reach a point where I can work my mistakes into the pattern of my life. Those parts of my life that I can't seem to accept and integrate will, I hope, come to fit into the larger fabric when viewed from a distance.

The memory of this quilt gives me hope that I may one day offer the tapestry of my life to a Higher Power who will say, "Well done. Only God is perfect."

United States

Has Al-Anon helped me to stop striving for perfection?

I Read a Poem As If It Were a Prayer

Early in recovery I had expected a personal relationship with a traditional divine being and, I am embarrassed to admit, actually prayed for that until my sponsor asked me when I was going to stop telling God what to do. Instead of feeling enormously hurt by his remark—an old, familiar reaction pattern of mine—I settled into a routine of praying only for the knowledge of God's will, as Al-Anon's Eleventh Step suggests. I can't say exactly when I became aware of feeling the presence of something both powerful and comforting, but I first noticed a heightened awareness when outdoors hiking or watching the sunset.

For me the validity of a spiritual awakening is confirmed by actual experience—that is, when I feel or sense something in my body rather than just think it in my mind. Still, it was a big surprise when I began to have profoundly moving experiences while reading poetry. Friends in the program helped me to overcome my usual insecurity and doubts about these experiences and encouraged me to enroll in a nearby university in order to study modern American poets presented as successors to nineteenth-century Romantics.

Gradually, I began to confirm in me what Keats called "the holiness of the Heart's affections and the truth of the Imagination."[1] Lately I have come to see that reality is more than just the everyday tangible things of our earthly existence.

More and more I have experienced an inner sense of truth and rightness when in contact with beauty, whether in art or nature. I have come to call that a form of conscious contact with the God of my understanding because it often seems as if I were with the best of friends or lovers. Like other relationships, this one is a changing and growing one. Above all, it defies detailed description and all attempts on my part to control it. Yet, I treasure the gift of being able, in my quiet time in the morning, to read a poem as if it were a prayer to that friend.

United States

When have I felt inspired by works of imagination?

[1] *John Keats*, edited by Elizabeth Cook ©1987. By permission of Oxford University Press.

An Art Exhibit

A few years ago my wife, stepfather and I attended an exhibition of paintings by an artist whose work especially appealed to my wife. I went without any great expectations, but when we arrived I realized that I was looking at a special collection.

The art had a dreamlike quality that seemed to express an inner experience of real exuberance and love. I found that even the exhibition rooms seemed to radiate a deep, almost meditative sense of pleasure and even pride in the expansive nature of the work. Even my stepfather, a talkative and impatient man, seemed pleased to spend some quiet time in the presence of these paintings.

I remember that afternoon as a day when I felt a great sense of peace and acceptance. I see those moments, when we stood in silence with those paintings in a special light, as a gift from a Higher Power. Even to recall the experience is to be restored, ever so gently, to sanity.

United States

In what ways has Al-Anon deepened my appreciation for creativity?

Chapter 5

Faith and Spirituality

One obvious area of spirituality not mentioned in Al-Anon is religion. However, throughout humanity's history, religious practice has been the most visible expression of spiritual experience.

It is not surprising, then, that some Al-Anon members find areas of spiritual experience in observing their religious beliefs, while other members choose not to be affiliated with a specific religion or choose a new religion. And perhaps, despite the differences in specific religious tenets, we can discern at least one common thread. As one religious leader has put it, "My true religion is kindness."

Early Spiritual Experience

My doorway to spirituality was my religious experience. Before I had any broader sense of the spiritual, I worshipped regularly and enthusiastically. While I enjoyed participating with others of my faith, I found myself drawn to private prayer and meditation in our place of worship.

The more I sat alone with my religious experience, the more often I found myself reflecting that I seemed to be practicing a new form of prayer and meditation, one that put me in touch with a Higher Power not contained within the practices and beliefs of my religion. As time passed, the spiritual content of my experiences became more clearly separated from my religious practice, and eventually I came to depend on my personal sense of a Higher Power for the guidance and direction that previously I had found in my religion. Eventually I came to feel that my religion served for me much as training wheels had served when I was learning to ride a bicycle. When I realized I could keep my own balance, I found it desirable to remove the wheels.

In Al-Anon my sense of gratitude for my religious participation has only deepened, for I have come to appreciate more fully the central importance of my early introduction to spiritual experience.

United States

Using Al-Anon principles, what doors to spirituality have opened for me?

A New Respect

One area in which my spiritual life in Al-Anon has changed my experience dramatically is religion. I still do not practice the formal religion of my family but I no longer view it with resentment. I am able to accept and even embrace its spiritual message and to join with others occasionally for religious practice with a feeling of respect and even appreciation. While I may not have "come home" to my family's religion in any committed way, I have no problem going home for the holidays.

When I visit, I no longer see ceremonies based on dogma and celebrants who I thought were exclusive and judgmental. Instead, I see rituals of worship and celebration and people trying to practice a way of life based on love and trust.

Thanks to my Al-Anon experience, I know what these people seek. Again, thanks to my Al-Anon experience, I know that together in these religious practices as in other places where there is willingness, we may hope to find what we seek.

United States

Have I learned to respect individual religious differences within others?

It Works for Me

A friend once said, "Religion is for those who are afraid of going to hell and spirituality is for those who have already been there." That remark made me think. Since my teens I had been searching everywhere for safety and love, including in the church. I found religion, but very little spirituality. I prayed to God but I felt that He wasn't listening because He didn't answer in the ways I expected. Of course, I had all the solutions which I delivered to God in my "prayers."

My life turned further and further away from the church and I became more and more unhappy and worried. My father's alcoholism was increasing slowly but steadily, and the whole family focused on searching for solutions while hiding our problems from others.

Finally, I found Al-Anon. They started to talk about a "Power greater than ourselves," about God. "Oh no," I thought, "I don't want this!" The first time I read the Serenity Prayer I left out the first word, "God," but I couldn't think who else could give me serenity.

Slowly and carefully I began again to search for spirituality because I had already been to hell! I let go of tiny, tiny items to God, and I prayed small, careful prayers that couldn't "hurt" or change anything big. It took a year in Al-Anon before I dared to try living with a Higher Power and it took another year before I began to feel comfortable being together with my Higher Power. Now yet another year has passed and we have had our fights, God and I. I have quarreled with Him, doubted Him, and finally trusted Him. I have realized that my solutions may not always be best. I have come to understand that the passage of time can be a solution.

Sometimes I hand a problem over to God but the next morning I take it back, twist and turn it, worry, and try to find a solution. I have to say to myself, "Don't! Just Let Go and Let God!" More and more, I trust my Higher Power.

And so I came back to religion. I felt drawn back to the church but I didn't know how it fit in with my newfound spirituality. I found that it works splendidly. I act at church as at an Al-Anon meeting: I take what I like and leave the rest. Now I can go to church without being bothered by specific teachings. I can grow in my spirituality and find friendship, as in Al-Anon.

Still, it is in Al-Anon I have found my Higher Power and the courage to trust Him. It is in Al-Anon that my spirituality has its roots. At church I can widen my horizons. That is how Al-Anon works for me.

Sweden

How has my spiritual experience in Al-Anon influenced my view of my religious experiences?

Prayer

The Serenity Prayer and the slogan "Let Go and Let God" helped a lot in changing my attitude. When I realized I can only change myself and I am powerless over others, things began to happen and my struggle ended. So many people in this world are facing the problem of alcoholism, but all are not Al-Anon members. I am privileged to be a member only because there is a Power greater than I am. God wants me to grow in this program and to cope with the problem. I was so involved with the alcoholic and not in a position to manage my own life. My situation made me search for a Higher Power.

I have a personal name for my God. I worship Him and pray to Him. When unwanted thoughts come to my mind, I divert my mind by singing songs. The attitude that nothing is permanent in this world and that I have been born alone and will die alone has helped me to know about the reality of life.

When I am confused and depressed, I pass my problems to God. It is a miracle my problems would be solved in a better way, as God knows what is best for me. Whenever I trust God and surrender to Him, He has really helped.

Sometimes I fear when my husband drives a vehicle on the national highway when he is fully drunk. I pray to God to take care of him. Then I sensibly think that by worrying I can't prevent anything from happening. Next day my husband comes home in a very good condition. It is really a miracle. This type of spiritual attitude, leaving everything to God and surrendering completely to Him, has helped me in relieving tension.

India

Have I tried prayer to relieve tension in my life?

Finding My Own Way

A few years ago I felt I was at a stopping place. With his compulsive drinking my husband of 20-some years had disappointed me for the last time. I had no more respect for him or myself for staying in this marriage and I gave him an ultimatum: "Quit drinking and go to AA or the kids and I are leaving." There was no big surprise how that turned out. He went to AA for about once or twice a week due to my dragging him and then he said, "I've had enough. I'm not an alcoholic and I have nothing in common with those people."

Very luckily my brother-in-law, who had been trying to help both of us, told me about Al-Anon. I went expecting these people to tell me how to tell my husband not to drink. I know I cried at every meeting for at least the first month. We read the Steps every week. They were just as clear as mud till I started taking them, picking them apart one at a time.

The *One Day at a Time In Al-Anon* book has been my true guide to understanding what I'm doing and my own responsibility. Whenever he "falls off the wagon," I go back to Step One, rethink the wisdom in that Step and let the old feelings of anger and "How dare you do this to me?" roll off my back. I know this will be a lifelong trial of making each step come true for me, but each challenge has made me see the true serenity that I can achieve.

In Step Two, I had a personal challenge to overcome. Uncomfortable with the religious practices of my childhood, I felt I needed to be truly aware of what I was praying to. After several months of combing the library for religious material, I found a book by a leader of another belief. I read the introduction and had to read it over again and again. It was so clear and familiar, as if he were talking about me and my most personal thoughts.

Through many more like sources, I found my true path. A year and a half ago I dedicated myself in a personal ceremony to follow my spiritual path. There is one basic law I like: If you harm no one, do what you will.

I believe other worlds exist around us that are not physical but spiritual in nature, and communication between them and us is possible. I celebrate the important dates of nature, including the solstices and equinoxes and every full and new moon.

The Serenity Prayer takes on a little different meaning as well. I believe that I am greatly empowered by my gods and this prayer is a very good reminder to use my goddess-given intelligence.

My husband doesn't understand what Al-Anon has done for me personally, only that I can find reasons to smile now. That really wasn't possible before, when all I could see was a brick wall called divorce. He tries not to drink but when he does it doesn't overshadow my own self-worth. I think I have found who I really am through my own personal search and Al-Anon; I like myself. Others around me are assets now, not liabilities.

I know that my beliefs are not for many people. It does not recruit others. It's for those who are born with the curiosity for it. My husband still believes as I once did and that's fine. We all must follow our own paths. Like death and one's own opinion, it must be ours alone.

United States

How has Al-Anon supported my spiritual growth?

Praying with Others

One of the perennial sources of spiritual renewal in my life is the experience of prayer in a group with people of faith. It is not just prayer that helps in my days but prayerfulness, by which I mean being receptive in prayer. Worshipping with others opens this space of prayerfulness for me and strengthens my sense of spiritual experience.

As I know from Al-Anon, people gathering together work miracles—which is to say that things happen that nobody could plan. Being together with others of like mind in a place of worship gives me permission to be in the moment in a new way—and as I have heard it said in Al-Anon, God works in the moment.

Cultivating prayerfulness in worship with others renews my contact with the bedrock of my spiritual experience.

United States

In my Al-Anon meetings do I sense shared spirituality?

My God Has Changed

I have been a member of a religious order since 1962, and have graduate and post-graduate degrees in theology. I first joined Al-Anon in 1988 because my life had become unmanageable due to living and working with people affected by alcoholism. No academic degrees or years of spiritual direction and training had prepared me for the turmoil of the disease of alcoholism. But those years had given me an openness and a willingness to admit my desperation and my need for help. I also had a habit of placing my life in God's hands. I joined Al-Anon with the readiness of a dry sponge.

In Al-Anon my God seemed to change as fast as I was changing. The Steps presented a spiritual path that had me start all over again as a child, to know myself and my God in ways I never dared to before. First of all, in taking Step One I had to admit my own primary and secondary addictions, admit how much I created and enjoyed the role of victim, caretaker, etc. My relationship with God, therefore, changed drastically. In doing Steps Four and Five, I felt a keen compunction—that is, sorrow mixed with a tremendous sense of being loved and accepted just as I am. This God of love came to me through members in the program. I continue to see clearly how my family of origin affected my understanding of myself and my relationships. God loves me as I am.

There has been a tremendous peace that has come with accepting myself as a member of the human race, no longer trying to be and appear perfect. Spirituality is basically this: I am at peace and in harmony with myself, with God, with others, with nature. I no longer feel as if life is a battle in which I am trying to change everything and everyone.

There is acceptance of the imperfections in myself, in others, in nature, and so much to learn. God guides me.

Another dimension of my spirituality that has changed so much is my relationships. I had to be the center of attention and in my own mind, I was. I blamed everyone else for my misery and approval was essential to my own self-worth. The program is causing a profound change. I find myself being genuinely interested in others for their own sake, not for what they can bring me. I feel responsible, not for others' happiness, but for healthy boundaries in my relationships. God is changing me.

Al-Anon has given me the people I need to be as honest with myself and others as I possibly can. Mature spirituality is this: breaking down one self-deception after another, having a genuine sense of being at one with wounded human beings, and rejoicing in the emptiness and longing—making room for God. The spiritual path of the Twelve Steps, and the spiritual support of the program have turned my life upside down and inside out, but with it is a tremendous freedom that comes with minding my own business—changing the things I can, in myself—and in doing so, seeing God, myself, others, and the world with more love than I ever thought possible. God frees and empowers me.

Canada

How has my spirituality affected my self-worth?

Chapter 6

Affirmation Through Other People

According to an African proverb, "A person is a person because of other people."

Much of our spiritual experience, when we come to look for it, is spoken by others—friends, relatives, even strangers. Especially in Al-Anon we are blessed by contact with many members of varied spiritual experience. As we develop a willingness to be receptive, we find unexpected wisdom and guidance in the words and actions of those around us. Overlooked and forgotten memories, chance meetings, brief snatches of conversation can all lead to moments that remind us of the workings of a Higher Power in our daily lives.

Learning To Love

Over twenty years ago my husband reached his bottom and he had to be hospitalized in a mental institution. He was released after twenty days and his sobriety began. I began to visit him. Here is when my struggle against my fantasies began. I fell in to a bottomless hole in which I didn't know what to do with my life, since to this point I had always lived my life for my husband and children.

He was active in AA and he began to become responsible. My children grew and they no longer needed me as much. After all, I still didn't know how to live my life. In this manner ten years elapsed, each day my husband got better, and I got worse. I had to reach my own bottom. After a great personal and matrimonial crisis, I reached a decision to attend Al-Anon.

I arrived at Al-Anon destroyed and feeling as if I were in a hole because my life was in chaos. I felt that everyone in the group had worse problems because most of their spouses were still drinking. All I wanted to know was what I needed to do in order for my husband to listen to me once again. Three months passed before I heard the message.

After that moment, I tried to do everything the members suggested. I saw that the program worked for them and I thought to myself, "then why not for me?" I began by choosing a sponsor and, after completing an inventory of my life, I started to work on the program. I received compensation. Since that time ten years have elapsed, with me being a member of Al-Anon and my husband in AA.

I am not going to tell everything that transpired during this time because it has been a lot of things, some good, some not so good. The good thing is that we celebrated our 25th wedding anniversary recently by renewing our vows in the same church in which we were married the first time, surrounded by our children, parents, brothers and sisters. It was a beautiful ceremony. We were dressed in our wedding attire with our children as witnesses.

We received a lot of gifts but the most important one this time was loving one another without asking anything in return. It was a gift knowing that we desire to be together, for whatever time is remaining, with both our defects and virtues. We know that we are not perfect—but who is? Later we had a great banquet and a fantastic honeymoon. We went to San Francisco, Los Angeles, Honolulu, and Washington. It was a dream come true. But the most important thing—and words cannot express what I feel inside—is that we owe everything to AA and Al-Anon.

In ending, all I can say is that I am happy. I would like to tell those persons who are still suffering not to doubt. Be happy if possible. You can attain it. We had all the prerequisites for a bad outcome, but here we are, more in love than ever before. With all my respect for those persons reading this, I would like to tell you that this is the experience of two people whose lives crossed the disease of alcoholism. With the program and much love, we can live a good life.

Spain

How has Al-Anon helped me to recognize love in my life?

Here Was Love

I've been in the fellowship now for over seven years. When I started coming to Al-Anon, both my marriage and my business were falling apart. I was totally selfish, obsessed with getting what I wanted. Scratch the surface and I was full of guilt and shame; scratch a bit deeper and there was this extremely strong, deep, fundamental belief in my own "wrongness" that I was separate from, and worse than, everybody else. This has felt as if it were at the core of my being ever since age twelve.

And it's all changing—really changing. I am getting to understand the world is not actually divided into two groups—everybody else and me. I don't have to cover up the real me and constantly pretend. I do not have to manipulate to get what I want and unimportant decisions are not matters of life and death.

This looseness, this relaxed feeling seeping into my life, is spiritual. Once, in order to feel good, I needed to be making lots of money, be very impressive, or be gratifying my appetites. I don't have anything against these things, but now I often feel good without them simply because I'm living my day well. It's free, no strings—and I always thought I had to try so hard to get it. I think having children helped to wise me up—here was love, both from and to me, pure and unmanipulated. For the first time in me, the disease was confronted.

And so sometimes, just sometimes, all my worries, concerns and priorities fade, life quiets down, and I am living my day as God made me, in God's world. And there is such peace and strength in this. For this I thank God and I thank the fellowship.

Australia

How have other in the Al-Anon fellowship helped me
develop my spiritual values?

Chance Meetings

Sometimes I hear the voice of a Higher Power in chance meetings.

I recall a simple message that came to me last week. I was walking to a religious service after work and feeling pretty discouraged. When I walked by a doorman I see often, he greeted me and said, "You need to stand up! Stand up straight!" I walked on past another doorman, who also gave me a friendly greeting and then said almost the very same words, "Stand up, you need to stand up!" I had my message for the day—a simple one: Stand up, stand up!

These two familiar faces had given me the message I needed just to bring me back to the present and leave the rest of my problems in the hands of a Power greater than myself. Their prompting led me back to living One Day at a Time while letting go and letting God.

United States

Do I notice Al-Anon principles at work in unexpected places?

Friends

While talking to a friend about my current difficulties with my alcoholic family, I paused to wonder out loud what I might really want in my dealings with them. I was thinking small, along the lines of a comfortable strategy for managing the next twelve hours.

As I paused to think, my friend exclaimed in spontaneous exasperation, "What do you want? You want a loving, caring family!"

I felt a weight lift off my shoulders. She was right; that was what I wanted. I was no closer to having one, but I was suddenly reminded that I was struggling with an unmanageable situation. I was powerless over the effects of alcohol in my life and I had the option of looking for love and care from other, more reliable sources.

I felt that a "Power greater than ourselves" had suddenly spoken through my friend.

United States

**When has my Higher Power spoken to me
through other Al-Anon members?**

Instruments of My Higher Power

Before coming into Al-Anon 16 years ago, I felt a wall was being built up between God and me. The God of my understanding was important to me, but I felt He had turned against me. I certainly didn't deserve to be subjected to all the uncertainties I was facing in life. I hated getting out of bed in the morning because I felt so defeated, so low in self-esteem.

Then with the help of a loving, caring sister-in-law, I found Al-Anon. I firmly believe today that a Power greater than myself gave me the strength to attend my first meeting. I have been growing spiritually ever since. I came to know a Higher Power who assists me and gives me courage and love on a daily basis. I try to pray for guidance each day and give thanks to the God of my understanding each night. As I am human, I do not do this as often as I would like to.

I feel that all Al-Anon members are instruments of my Higher Power, assisting me in leading a healthier, saner life. A Power greater than myself has enabled me to meet each challenge in life with a positive, serene attitude, and I now make stepping stones out of stumbling blocks.

Canada

Can I explain the God of my understanding?

Working Together

When I was young, I used to spend some time with my grandparents. Because my grandfather was a surgeon, my grandmother had a weekly ladies' group that met at her house to fold dressings for the hospital where my grandfather worked.

These women, meeting with a common purpose that sustained them, acted with a grace, vitality, and humor that was uplifting. Within their group I felt a powerful energy much greater than that of the individual members.

They seemed to share a force that produced a mound of surgical dressings as an afterthought, while it also worked to transform the experience of the individual members.

Seeing this group in action was my earliest experience of a Higher Power emerging from the focus on a common goal. In the function of Al-Anon groups, I have come to know this feeling well.

United States

***Have I felt a Higher Power
working in my Al-Anon group?***

Expressing Love

Recently I attended the wedding of an old friend. While the wedding itself was a civil ceremony with no reference to any religious or spiritual tradition, the whole experience of witnessing and celebrating the declaration of this bond of love felt like a spiritual experience to me.

In Al-Anon, I see myself becoming more fully the person I have always wanted to be and this wedding gave me a golden opportunity to enjoy my progress. More clearly than ever before, I could feel the power of love at work in my life. I could feel a new assurance by celebrating the virtues of commitment and caring. What's more, I could see the ways in which my Al-Anon experience has helped me find the serenity, courage, and wisdom to express the love I feel for others. Now I can receive others' expressions of love for me.

In celebrating my friend's marriage, I found myself receiving from others the love and caring I was giving. In this group I felt a presence that was greater than that of the separate individuals, a gentle presence that spoke of the spiritual and inspired me to treat others with dignity, respect, and love.

United States

How has Al-Anon helped me to be gentle and loving with myself and others?

An Invitation from a Friend

I was told that I was born one beautiful sunny afternoon. I woke up to a world I didn't know yet, a world that held many surprises. My cradle, where so many came with fine presents, was for me a cradle wrapped with alcoholism. An only child, I couldn't share "the problem" with other brothers or sisters. As I grew I watched what my father did. I suffered a great deal, watching my mother always praying, making promises and crying in corners. At home there was always a silence, an emptiness, since we couldn't even speak with my father.

When special holidays arrived, as I still remember clearly, I saw other children getting presents. But I saw my father sleeping, as he was getting over a drunk and didn't even remember what day it was. The world would close in on us on a day like that, as my mother and I would feel only shame and loneliness. We didn't have friends. Who would want to visit an alcoholic house?

That's how I reached adolescence. I grew up with serious problems in school. Life for me was very difficult. What I wanted most at the time was for my father to die, which would be the only way my life and my mother's would be improved.

When I was a girl of only twelve, my father received treatment which had no effect. In a few days everything would start again. I would encounter danger in the streets, sometimes feeling fear, as it was a big city where I took him for the treatments. This happened eight times over 32 years of alcoholism. Seeing my home each time getting worse, I also started to go to parties.

Later on a door opened; someone arrived. The sun's rays penetrated inside the house. It was a friend who brought an invitation. I entrusted our lives to God and left in search of help.

It was a strong and beautiful light that would come to our path. A wonderful program that I would come to know, a treatment for me and my family. My father went to AA. He was ill. My mother and I went to Al-Anon. We, too, needed treatment.

There everything began to grow clear in our life. How difficult the first meetings were, as I was still upset, anguished, suffering from the past years. But there with my friends I began to like myself again and to like others. I forgave myself and loved my father again and those around me. At home, holy blessings flowed, much strength, courage to live anew. Thanks to this Higher Power whose help I asked for during many rainy nights. They were years of many appeals and prayers.

Today I can say I am the daughter of a recovering alcoholic, and happy. I learned much in this program, and I wish many other sons and daughters can have the courage to make this appeal to God. We know this program can save other lives. I live each day. I love the sick. I pass my days calmly.

I had forgotten how to pray, but today I have learned again; at night I give thanks for the alcoholic father I was able to help——the man I can call father today.

I love life, I love this program that one day changed my family.

Brazil

What friends have brought a strong light into my life?

A Lesson in Expressing Appreciation

While ordering a sandwich from a local delicatessen, I found myself appreciating the attentiveness and good nature of the woman taking my order. I had seen her in the neighborhood for years and I had always been impressed by her behavior. I began to consider the possibility of telling her my thoughts, of thanking her not just for my sandwich but for her care, cooperation and good spirits.

In a hurry to purchase a drink, I stepped away from the counter and let a friend collect the sandwiches. As I realized I had shied away from risking a personal comment, I also noticed that this woman had no other customers and that I had another chance to speak my mind.

"I'd just like to thank you for your cooperation and good spirits over the years here," I said—or something similar, but less coherent. At first she looked startled by my comment, and then pleased.

"Oh, thank you,'" she said. "It's a real joy to be here...sometimes." I realized as we shared a good-natured laugh that this woman had more depth than I had realized; that she had a good sense of humor, good timing, honesty, and tact, as well as a good attitude.

"Thank you very much," she said again. "You really made my day."

How privileged I felt, and how guided by spirit, to be prompted to give a little acknowledgment to a woman who so richly deserved it. In sharing a little sense of the caring I learned in Al-Anon, I had received so much in return. Simply ordering a sandwich had turned into food for thought for the week, and had strengthened my sense of a spiritual connection with another human being. What I had given had been returned to me with interest.

United States

When was the last time I went out of my way to say "Thank You?"

A Chance Remark

When playing doubles one week, my tennis partner remarked that speeding up the pace of his service game seemed to help his performance. I tried it myself and also had good results. "I see what you mean about speeding up the game," I said. He replied, "Yes, it's working today, but every time out is a clean slate."

I had never before heard any words of wisdom from my partner and I may never again, but his observation about tennis struck me as true for the rest of my life. In Al-Anon I learn and continually re-learn. I must seek the guidance of a Higher Power every day. Today's words of wisdom can come through to me from anyone, anywhere.

United States

Has a chance remark brightened my life recently?

Forgiveness

Sometimes my spiritual lessons come from unlikely sources. In this case I'm thinking of a sister with whom I have a difficult relationship. After corresponding with her at length about a family problem, I realized that we were making rapid progress in giving voice to our separate hurts, but no progress in solving the problem. What I viewed as her stubbornness and negativity forced me to examine my experience from a spiritual perspective.

I began in the usual place—powerlessness. I progressed to my next familiar but welcome destination—detachment. For the first time I noticed with great relief that I did not have to understand my sister in order to detach. Instead, I could just stop trying for the moment and feel confident that perhaps some day, if it were appropriate, I might understand her better. I had arrived at letting go and letting God, and I thought I'd reached my final destination, a spot where I felt passive and disengaged but still greatly relieved.

That very day I happened to read two brief articles—one on forgiveness and one on prayer. Quite unexpectedly, I felt another great release as I realized even still without understanding her, I could explore the idea of moving from detachment to the more active practice of forgiveness. In my experience, I had suffered hurts in dealing with my sister. By accepting my feelings, not as objective "truth" but as my experience, and detaching, I could now move beyond letting go of my resentments and take action by exercising forgiveness. I could picture my sister moving in a warm light, holding a bouquet, smiling and feeling at ease. At least on a spiritual level, I could release my painful past.

I then began to consider the article on prayer. It spoke of the power of prayer in healing and urged praying for others as well as oneself. Somehow this thought opened a new door in my experience of prayer and allowed me, as part of what felt like God's will for me, to pray for healing in my sister's life as well as my own.

Thanks to my sister's refusal to see things my way, I had stumbled upon a whole new spiritual province in which a passive sense of detachment blossomed into an active experience of forgiveness, and a disconnected sense of letting go was transformed into a committed vision of the power of prayer.

Through a difficult sister, my Higher Power had delivered a precious gift.

United States

*What lessons have I learned from difficult people that enhance my
Al-Anon experience?*

My Paper Bag God

When I first came to Al-Anon, I didn't like to hear the word God or the phrase Higher Power. It made me angry and uneasy (both great covers for confusion). Anyway, the people in my group gently explained that my Higher Power is a personal choice. I didn't have to believe or disbelieve in God to come to meetings. No one was going to force God down my throat. Each person is free to make his or her own choice. There is no right or wrong, just a personal choice.

I still was upset at the mention of the G-word. So I took a little time to think about it. Overall I liked the ideals expressed in Al-Anon and I needed the help. The God "thing" was upsetting, so I decided to separate the issues for the time being. I would take the program and let go of the "G-stuff" until I was ready to deal with it. I would neither accept nor reject, believe nor disbelieve, just listen and turn off what was upsetting. "Take what you like and leave the rest." As my life settled down, I took time to explore my thoughts and feelings on God. First Things First.

At 30-plus years old I was still trying to believe in the big guy in the sky from Sunday school or in somebody else's God. Through listening, I have discovered that even people in the same church envision God differently. God is a personal vision.

I felt like people were trying to give me their God, and as if they were cramming it down my throat. Through Al-Anon, I've met people who were willing to put their God on the table for me to look at and even pick up and hold if I wanted. All without pressure to keep it or accept it or anything!

I didn't believe in God but "something" is very real. If I took a brown paper bag and could extricate that inexplicable joy and caring that I see in each person and place it in the bag and shake it up, there would be a Higher Power, as real as you or I.

It is impossible to take that "specialness" from each person and reassemble it into something tangible, but that does not diminish its existence or spirit.

For me there is no big guy in the sky. It's as if the paper bag containing God has been sprinkled all over the earth, and each and every living thing has been touched. We all carry that spark of goodness and caring. Some people try to bury it, but it is there—however difficult to see. Others have a brightly burning flame. Most have a pretty decent pilot light! Whatever, it is there.

I see it in kindness, caring smiles, tears, birds singing, an unexpected happening, meetings, in Mother Nature and so much more. In all people and in all things there is a genuine worth that, if extracted and piled together, is God. He is very real.

No one person, place, or thing is God. He is an intangible essence or spirit filling our world.

I accept that you may have a different perspective on God. I hope you will find a little tolerance for my "Paper Bag God."

Canada

Where have I seen this caring spark?

Chapter 7

Spiritual Recovery in Al-Anon

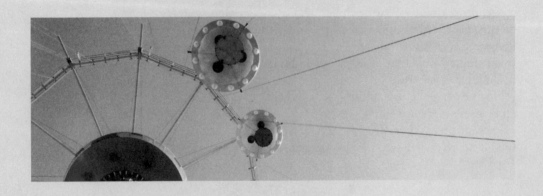

At Al-Anon's First International Convention in Montreal, Lois W. stated, "I don't think there is a spiritual part of the program. I think Al-Anon is a spiritual program. Every activity can have a spiritual motive."[1]

In Al-Anon we share our experiences in order to gain a common strength and hope. Here members relate their personal observations and their involvement in a search for a Higher Power. The individual events, feelings, and practices described are as diverse as our worldwide fellowship.

[1] First Steps—Al-Anon ...35 years of beginnings - p. 156

Al-Anon Groups

My first sense of a Higher Power in Al-Anon came through my most basic experience of the groups themselves. I noticed quite quickly that those in attendance (whom I had not yet learned to call "members") were trusting me with the true stories of their lives. When I dared to speak, I noticed that people listened with respect and allowed me to say whatever was on my mind.

I found myself in the midst of groups that treated me with trust and respect, though my experiences around alcoholism had led me to expect to be confronted with an underlying attitude of distrust and criticism, even if unspoken. What I noticed after my early encounters at Al-Anon meetings was that I left those meetings guided by a new sense of my own worth. The Higher Power in my life was the strength of the loving, caring person I was being encouraged to become.

United States

Have I felt the healing power of an Al-Anon group?

God with Skin

At a meeting I heard a loving story that has stuck with me.

There once was a little child who woke up in the middle of the night frightened and alone.

He ran to his parents' bed and crept closely between them.

His father said, "You know that when you woke up scared, God was with you."

The boy said, "I know, but I needed someone with skin!"

That's what Al-Anon is to many of us..."God with skin." He speaks to us through the loving words and shared experiences of the other members. He teaches us how to "hear" Him in their words, problems, and even coincidences in our lives.

When I need "God with skin"—I go to a meeting.

United States

What encounters with other Al-Anon members have given me spiritual guidance or helped me grow?

A Revitalizing Power

I have found many similarities in the teaching of Al-Anon and the teaching of respect for others that is the heartbeat of my heritage. Respect for our Mother Earth and for all kindred spirits, be they animal, rock, or human, is a priority.

Another area of similarity is in our meetings. My ancestors usually hold their ceremonies in circles. There is something sacred, ancient, and powerful in circles. I am not surprised, then, to remember we end most Al-Anon meetings in circles, holding hands and repeating prayers. In my Al-Anon home group we have our tables and chairs set in a circle, and I feel a spiritual connection as I look around into others' eyes to see the truth, love and sometimes sadness displayed there. Somehow getting in touch with others in this way helps me to focus on the group as a whole and on each member in turn.

When one of us speaks of his or her Higher Power during meetings, I feel a surge of energy and a revitalizing power fill the room. I feel it again as we hold hands in our closing circles. I have read about and talked to many Native Americans who recount this same phenomenon in their celebrations and clan gatherings. They say they get their individual strength from the coming together of their clan members, and that it sustains them until they meet again.

I feel the same about my Al-Anon meetings! I feel a wonderfully ancient yet ever-youthful universal force is at work in our world and my heart leaps for joy that I am a part of it. My people know that the Great Spirit is within us and I know an Indian walks in me...one who seeks to be whole in strength and spirit...to find the serenity and peace we all need. I know I will find all these things in the rooms of Al-Anon and in the unconditional love there that is the fertile ground in which I can grow.

United States

Do I feel a Higher Power working in the meetings I attend?

A Power in the Room

When I was growing up, our family attended church services sporadically, mostly to enjoy the music, but religion never played a big part in my life. I married a person of a different persuasion, and he, too, was casual about attending church.

When alcoholism reared its ugly head, I tried going back to my church for help, but didn't find it.

After many years looking for help, I eventually found Al-Anon and was attracted to the fellowship immediately. However, in trying to work Steps Three, Five, Six, Seven, and Eleven, I could not accept the God of my childhood.

I continued to attend meetings and came to believe there was a Power in the room and no matter what it was, I was getting great help from the sharings of others working the Twelve Steps.

I am thankful that today I can look back and say with gratitude that attending this program and giving service to Al-Anon gave me a wonderful and fulfilling way of life. I now accept that there is a spiritual power—but not one that is more than human.

Ireland

What is my personal version of a Power greater than myself?

Encouragement To Look

Much of what I needed in order to find my version of a Higher Power was simply encouragement to look for one. I found much of that encouragement in the fundamental structure of the Al-Anon groups I attended. I noticed that no authority was present and no one had any plans to become one or to invite one to visit.

The program had suggestions but no doctrine. It had guideposts but no guides. It had members but no authorities. It encouraged me to realize that I was the single person who knew my story best and that, while I might not be able to find answers for others, I could become well-equipped to find answers for myself.

The simple invitation to participate fully in finding my own version of a Higher Power was, in itself, a spiritual experience.

United States

How did I define my Higher Power when I first came to Al-Anon?

This Vital Force

My heritage is one of using circles for many rituals and ceremonies. The dances, drumming, singing and celebrating are always done in a circular pattern, as are ceremonies for peace. In our Al-Anon groups, I feel this vital force that is very strong whenever the mention of a Higher Power occurs, and especially at times when we hold hands or hold waists at closing circles or sharing circles.

The deep message of respect for other people, fellow creatures on our earth with us, and the interconnection we all are part of is another clear message, one which the Al-Anon program only helps enhance as a part of the whole picture brought to us down through the ages. I think there is a real need for people to get back to these ancient feelings and practices and I am so happy to be a part of it through Al-Anon.

United States

How has Al-Anon strengthened my spiritual beliefs?

Opening to New Ideas

When I first came to Al-Anon I was so thoroughly lost and confused that not even talk of God could frighten me away. While going to meetings and reading Al-Anon literature I hung on, knowing that I could take what I liked about spirituality and leave the rest. Listening to others and reading *As We Understood...* helped open my eyes to the great diversity of spiritual pathways in the program.

My awakening from a spiritual coma began when it finally dawned on me that in Al-Anon it really was all right to have a God of my very own understanding. To me, it was a revolutionary idea that I had a choice. I could have a Higher Power that was adequate for my personal needs.

For a while, Al-Anon became for me the equivalent of a spiritual shopping mall where I could try on all sorts of spiritual dress until I found an ensemble that I really liked for myself. Correspondingly, as trust in my own judgment grew, I became less and less fearful of others' spiritual outfits and their various concepts of a Higher Power, no matter how outlandish their views seemed to me.

Today, I keep going to Al-Anon meetings and feel confident that I will be accepted. I stay open to new ideas and know that my personal spiritual journey will continue to unfold.

Canada

**Has fear kept me from finding
a Higher Power?**

Feeling Better Without Knowing Why

One of my first experiences of a Higher Power working in my Al-Anon life was very simple: I felt better after meetings than I did before. I wasn't really sure why. What's more, I found I didn't necessarily care why I felt better, especially on the days when I felt a great deal better, the days when I felt like talking, smiling and laughing.

My idea of being guided by a Power greater than myself was that I now had a general plan to sit down in Al-Anon meetings a few times a week, confident I would often feel better leaving than I did when I arrived. What a reassuring difference in my week!

United States

Do I recognize the simple ways my Higher Power helps me?

Trust

Looking back on my years in Al-Anon, I see that my first task in finding a Higher Power that suited my needs was strengthening my ability to trust. In the alcoholic home of my childhood, I had learned that I could trust no one, perhaps least of all myself. I clung tightly to the practice of trying to manipulate and control others, chiefly by pleasing them.

The growth of my spiritual trust had three distinct stages. First, I began by learning to trust the Al-Anon program and the people in it. I found that by reading the literature and listening to members, I actually was being encouraged to find the God of my very own understanding. I felt free to start trusting my own experience in spiritual matters.

In the second stage of my growth while I continued to listen to others and to read spiritual material, I began to explore my own ideas. I was able to come to an understanding of a Higher Power I could trust. I had arrived at a spiritual trust that told me I could let go of my desire to control others and let my God have control. In completing this second stage, I needed to take the concept of "understanding" in Step Three quite literally. The free use of my imagination, along with continued listening and reading, led me to an understanding of God, a knowledge of God, that was adequate for my human needs.

Now, in the third stage of spiritual trust, I realize as I share with others that my personal understanding of God changes continually as I change. Furthermore, I have begun to trust the process of trust itself. As I change and progress in the program, as I learn about my God every day, I am learning to let go of control on a continual basis.

I know now that my understanding of God—even my personal God—will never be complete. Just as my understanding of myself will never be complete. I grow and change constantly. What is becoming increasingly real to me, therefore, is acceptance, a sense of humanness, of my limitations as a child of God. I am neither super-human—in control of others—nor sub-human—in others' control. The gift I have received from Al-Anon has been the gift of self.

Canada

In what ways has Al-Anon helped me to trust my own experience?

———◆———

Special Kindness

When I first came to Al-Anon, I didn't just have problems with someone else's drinking. My mother was dying of cancer and I was distraught. At my first meeting I talked about my plight and all of the difficult decisions I had to make about my mother's care. I felt crushed by my responsibilities.

After the meeting an older woman approached me to express her concern and to reassure me. After we had talked a bit, she said to me, "You know, your mother has a Higher Power, too." Hearing that sentence was my first spiritual experience in the program. I felt a huge weight lift from my shoulders as I realized that I could love and care for my mother without feeling that I was in charge of her illness.

I could feel the force of a Power greater than myself in this homespun observation, and I have never forgotten that member's kindness.

United States

How has Al-Anon helped me find relief in troubling situations?

———◆———

Crossing Barriers

Al-Anon has been a way of life for me since I joined. The program has definitely reconnected and enhanced my spiritual growth.

Growing up in a culture where admitting powerlessness essentially made me less than a man prevented me from seeking help for a long time. Being an ethnic Chinese, I found it shameful to admit loss of control in my life. I believe denial is a characteristic of my culture and I thought that accepting my powerlessness would make me lose face. Living at times in a small town in the Bible Belt deep south of the United States and being involved in a gay relationship added further barriers that made it difficult for me to consider seeking help.

Somehow when the pain was too much to bear, I crossed all my mental barriers and attended an Al-Anon meeting. It was a matter of life or death and embarrassment was not going to kill me. I could not hide the color of my skin, but I could hide my sexuality. Slowly I gained the courage to tell my secret to a few members, who still loved me the same. Those who truly practice their program and have gone through life's darkest moments did not have any reservations about accepting me. Those were the ones I spiritually connected with and I gained confidence and strength from them.

I became very active in service work as my group's representative. I still have not found more than one or two Asian members in the program. I have attended a few large conventions in the South but have felt sad to see very few members of Asian background. I am glad to have stayed in the program. Through it, I have met a great many people with whom I would never otherwise cross paths in my daily life. I thank Al-Anon for letting me voice my experience. I hope it will help other minorities to join the   program.

Canada

*What emotional barriers to spirituality have
I crossed to find my place in Al-Anon?*

A Favorite Reading

For a long time, I felt uncomfortable with my version of spirituality. I struggled; I really struggled with it. I felt pretty defiant, the way I felt about many things. Growing up with alcoholism had taught me to distrust the wisdom and help offered to me.

Then I heard a member recommend a page in *One Day at a Time in Al-Anon*, one she said she read every day, and that she said had changed her life. It was September 2nd, and part of it says: "If I try each day to put my point of view and my attitudes on a sound spiritual basis, I know it will change all the circumstances of my life for the better, too." [1]

I had trouble with the lines at the end, so for a while I just left that part off. Its religious association was not helpful to me, and the rest of the page made sense without it.

I don't know whether reading that page was my spiritual awakening, but it very definitely got me thinking about applying Al-Anon to my daily life and putting my life on a sound spiritual basis.

United States

What passages in our literature give me special reassurance?

[1] *One Day at a Time in Al-Anon* p. 246

Words

I came to Al-Anon by an unusual route. An unfamiliar but deep feeling of hate forced me to seek help. Feeling exhausted both spiritually and physically, I found the road out of my dead end after taking a course about psychic power. I returned to my faith and dared to turn to God with my thoughts and with my voice. I learned to find my true self, to listen to the voice of my conscience and to be led by its suggestions.

At this time I became familiar with Al-Anon's literature. After reading it, I comprehended that it is most magnificent and practical. It was as if these words melted within me. I didn't need to look for words to express my thoughts; they were already written. Thank you, dear friends, for willingly sharing your experiences with those of us who still do not understand ourselves, with those of us who virtually carry the weight of all of the alcoholic's problems on our shoulders. Al-Anon's ideas, principles and program provide the road to spiritual progress.

Lithuania

What Al-Anon literature do I turn to for spiritual growth?

Useful Reminders

Sometimes my experience of a Power greater than myself is simply a nudge to maintain my sense of balance. I often get that nudge from Al-Anon literature. For example, these words from the leaflet on Detachment: "Detachment is neither kind nor unkind." Simple words, but so helpful. I carry this leaflet in my wallet for easy reference.

More recently I have found great consolation in these words from *Courage to Change - One Day at a Time in Al-Anon II*: "Being human is not a character defect!"[1] Again simple words that help me balance my own daily experience.

Part of my spiritual health depends on hearing reminders not to play God. Just keeping the focus on myself and doing the best I can helps me to leave room in my day for guidance. Our literature helps me remember my human limits—and my spiritual needs.

United States

What piece of Al-Anon literature has been most affective in my life ?

[1] *Courage to Change - One Day at a Time in Al-Anon II* - p. 151

The Twelve Steps

One of the most obvious Al-Anon experiences that gives me a feeling of guidance from a Higher Power is using the Twelve Steps themselves. This framework gives me release from the cunning, baffling, and powerful disease of alcoholism—a release I had been unable to accomplish through my own efforts. Working the Steps gives me access to a wisdom greater than any I have previously known.

As a result, I have been led to a way of life that provides me with a feeling of fulfillment. I face each day with a more constant assurance that I am a useful person. I see more clearly my responsibility and its limits. I treat myself and others with more respect and compassion.

I see in these changes the fruits of accepting the guidance of a Power greater than myself as expressed in the framework of the Twelve Steps themselves.

United States

How has using the Twelve Steps strengthened my relationship with my Higher Power?

Just a Couple of Words

It was 1984. Six weeks previously I had left my husband of 29 years to rot of his alcoholism in a South Pacific paradise. I had returned to Australia with the youngest of our seven children. She and I went to stay with another of my daughters who had recently heard of an organization called Al-Anon. Thinking it might help her mother, she took me along to a meeting.

Even in my confusion and misery I felt like a dry sponge soaking up water. I heard so much with which I could identify that it was incredible. I felt so much love (a stranger actually hugged me) that I didn't think I could contain it all. I took home numerous pamphlets and just devoured them—almost unable to comprehend that I had met other people who had been suffering just as I had all these years and longer.

I badly wanted to buy a copy of *One Day at a Time in Al-Anon* there and then, believing that if I could only have that book I would have enough wisdom to get on with the rest of my life. But some mean (wise) person insisted it would be better if I waited awhile and came to some more meetings first. (Thank you, oh wise person!)

Instead, I took home that night just a couple of words from that day's reading—August 4th—that kept repeating themselves in my poor muddled head: "accept" and "expect." How similar they sound but how different their meanings! "Accept" is the goodie. "Expect" is the baddie.

I began that evening my long, arduous, but very rewarding journey along the road that is Al-Anon. I realized that I had never "accepted" that my husband was an alcoholic, although I had known this for almost twenty-nine years. Because I wanted this so much, I kept on "expecting" him to stop drinking, along with all sorts of other behaviors that I expected of him so that I could be happy.

I have learned about and picked up more tools in this program since then and I have used them to the best of my ability, but this for me is one of the most useful. So I am still learning One Day at a Time to "accept" that my husband is an alcoholic and not to "expect" him to be my very own, custom-built Prince Charming. Acceptance is leading me inevitably toward serenity and a great sense of contentment in my life.

Australia

How has acceptance helped me overcome the effects of alcoholism?

The Steps Have Led Me To My Higher Power

The principles of this program and the Twelve Steps have led me to my Higher Power whom I prefer to call God. This I accomplished with the help of the Second and Third Steps. Trusting another human being by taking the Fifth Step gave me freedom from my past. The Sixth and Seventh Steps helped me trust my Higher Power in every area and every situation of my life. The Eighth and Ninth Steps gave me the courage to make amends to those I have hurt. What relief and acceptance I felt when I embraced and made amends to the person I had hurt the most—me. The Eleventh Step is my favorite. Each day brings me closer to my Higher Power by my praying, placing each day in His care.

It was my spiritual awakening to apply these Steps in my life. I need this program even more today than I did before. I have learned to speak a new language, the language of love. I have finally learned to take it home with me, where it belongs.

Iceland

How do I use this spiritual program in other aspects of my life?

The Twelve Traditions

For me, the essence of spiritual experience is feeling a force of protection and guidance in my life. I find one of the special, often underappreciated, sources of this feeling in our program's Twelve Traditions. Experiencing them in practice and learning to apply them myself has developed within me a deeper sense of confidence. Putting these principles into practice has given me contact with a flow of respect and compassion that was blocked before Al-Anon.

Focusing on the Traditions has given me a clear picture of my connection to Al-Anon's past, and its future. I see a bright path of healing directed by the Traditions that stretches back to this program's beginning and continues forward into the unforeseeable future.

Wherever this experience of protection and guidance comes from, I often feel it move into my life through the framework of our Traditions.

United States

What special guidance have I found in the Twelve Traditions?

I See Myself As a Vital Instrument

Before I came into the Al-Anon program, I was on a quest for a Power greater than myself through religion. I was paying too much attention to the human part, however, and not enough to the spiritual part. If those religious people made a mistake, I was very disappointed and angry; I thought they were supposed to be perfect and I couldn't believe what they were teaching me. After a while I tried to gain faith by myself through the prayers I was taught, through penance and self-punishment, too. I was doing all these things to bargain with a God that I didn't believe in and I didn't even like. By trying so hard in this quest, my life became even more unmanageable and I felt more pain. Life didn't make any sense to me and it was empty. I felt like a boat without a captain that was drifting without direction in a big ocean. I was getting deeper and deeper into my pain, feeling inferior, different, and lonely.

When I got to Al-Anon and people were talking about a Higher Power, I started feeling rebellious. All those old feelings started to show and I was feeling very uncomfortable. But thanks to the service work I was doing, I could see better how my Higher Power was working in my life and in the lives of others. My fellow members helped me with this quest. Now I see myself as a vital instrument in an orchestra where God is the director and now I don't feel alone anymore. I know now that there are other people like me who can help me. Now I am grateful to my Higher Power for my mental health and my physical health.

I know that I need to be more spiritual, but at least I feel that He is my friend. I feel that friendship through my friends in the fellowship because they are with me in the good times and the bad times. My Higher Power loves me unconditionally, just as my Al-Anon friends do. He teaches me through my fellow members how to live a better life. He gives me the wisdom to know when I make mistakes, so I can fix them.

This quest for a Higher Power was a necessity for me and I did it out of faith. However, today I have a great deal of faith and I believe that my Higher Power is in control of my whole being.

Mexico

How has service helped me to get acquainted with my Higher Power?

The Three Legacies

Upon being asked to lead an assembly workshop on Al-Anon's Twelve Concepts of Service, I began meditating. To help me, I reduced in size and cut and pasted the Three Legacies (Al-Anon's Twelve Steps, Traditions and Concepts of Service) of our program onto one sheet of paper. I was amazed at the weave of the spiritual principles that have become so much a part of the fabric of my life since I started attending Al-Anon.

I can see my unmanageable life: those times when I think I have power. I can go down to surrendering to my Higher Power's care or across to see that a common welfare coming first brings healing. I have ultimate responsibility and authority which I then delegate to others. I love to watch spirituality unfold in my life and the lives of others.

For me, those 36 simple statements, along with the Warranties, are a spiritual foundation for living life One Day at A Time. As I look at them, my Higher Power reveals more and more about how God works for healing, no matter what the challenge.

Starting with admitting powerlessness and arriving at an awareness of spirituality in all that I see, I've found a healing path for recovering, a path that includes trusting that God is always at work. No matter where I live or how I define my Higher Power, these simple principles have brought healing to my life within the worldwide fellowship of Al-Anon. I am grateful.

United States

Where do I see the three legacies of Al-Anon at work in my recovery?

Service

During the United States' Civil War, President Abraham Lincoln was asked if he thought God was on the side of the North or the South. He replied: "The question, sir, is not whether God is on one side or the other, but rather, are we on God's side?"

I take this story as a personal reminder that my effort in Al-Anon has been ultimately to seek to align myself with the purpose of a Higher Power, rather than to align a Higher Power to my purpose. My focus is passing on the love, support, and understanding that I have received from a Power greater than myself. In Al-Anon, service work has been a direct and joyful way to do this. In passing on what I have received, I embrace more fully the working of a Higher Power in my life and I acknowledge that this Power comes through me, not from me. The more I give of the guidance I have received, the more open I become to receiving further guidance.

Through service, a Power greater than myself has worked to restore me to sanity.

United States

How has my Higher Power guided me in service work for Al-Anon?

The Slogans

Evidence of a Higher Power at work in my life has come from many unexpected sources. One of them is my changing attitude toward Al-Anon's slogans. At first I found them simple-minded, uninspiring, awkward and simplistic, but I noticed that old-timers seemed to use them with real feeling and enthusiasm. Keep It Simple, Easy Does It, One Day at a Time. "Whatever," I thought, wondering how such mini-sermons could apply to my life, which seemed complicated and exceptional to me.

Much to my surprise, I found these slogans popping into my head as I moved through the day. Just for Today. I found these gentle sayings replacing the usual angry, judgmental thoughts I tended to direct at myself and others.

I began to feel some awareness of what many in Al-Anon call God's time. I began to realize that the solution to my daily problems might be to lighten my load rather than to increase my effort. I could struggle less and still do well if I stopped trying to move mountains. Listen and Learn, Let Go and Let God. I came to believe that I could learn to find solutions to my life's problems simply by looking for the guidance of a Power greater than myself—even if that power spoke in a homespun, quiet voice that just said Live and Let Live.

United States

What slogans have special meaning for me?

The Serenity Prayer

I'm twenty and I'm one of the youngest members of our group. My uncle has problems with alcohol. My uncle doesn't live with my family (I mean, at the same apartment); that's why I don't feel that my situation is as bad as that of many women around me who live with alcoholics every day. But I realize quite well how wonderful life is for all members of our family including my aunt and cousin, when my uncle is sober, and what pain is here when he is drinking.

Thanks to Al-Anon, I learned that alcoholism is a disease and I admitted I am powerless over alcohol. It's really hard to admit it and to live without any hope and support, unless I have an understanding that there is a Power greater than ourselves.

I can say that I don't belong to any denomination. I don't go to church and I don't know enough prayers, but Al-Anon's Serenity Prayer helps me a lot. For one thing, it makes me feel great in my fellowship. When we pray together at the beginning and at the end of the meeting, I feel that we are all together, that our souls are together, too, and that we are eager to help each other. What's more, this feeling is much more powerful when I think that AA members—our uncles, husbands, sons, friends—have the same prayer and they join us even though we are not together in our meetings.

I can't say that I can describe my Higher Power clearly. It's something that knows everything, that can support and help us. When I'm frightened in my everyday life, somebody in my family has problems with health, or my uncle has a depression which can end in drinking, I try to speak to my Higher Power using the Serenity Prayer, especially the following part: "God grant me the serenity to accept the things I cannot change." It gives me power to overcome difficulties.

I want to add that our fellowship is like a Higher Power, too. It's the great feeling that there are reliable people who always can be attentive to me, who can help me and share their problems and thoughts with me. I'm thankful to Al-Anon for this great feeling.

Russia

How have I used the Serenity Prayer in my recovery?

Service Was a Turning Point

After much emotional upheaval, my husband and I had separated. However, a month after he went into a treatment center and joined AA, we started living together again. When I found Al-Anon, I was feeling sorry for myself, fearful of my husband, resentful, and absolutely frozen emotionally.

The atmosphere of the meetings was friendly, but I was very surprised to hear some of the women talk about loving their alcoholic husbands when I felt so ashamed for having fallen in love with such a faulty example of a human being.

One meeting a week was all I could handle because I didn't want others to see how bad I felt. The Steps, I thought, were only for long-time members. My first two years in the program were hard years of angry words and ice-cold silences between me and my husband.

I envied others in my group who talked about the wonderful changes after the alcoholic stopped drinking. I got angrier and angrier at him for not changing. By the grace of God, I kept going to meetings. One member became my sponsor. She encouraged me to forgive myself, to pour out all the anger and doubt.

Service was a turning point. At the Iceland National Conference I had my first spiritual awakening. Suddenly it all made sense. Listening to others opened my eyes. Those attending Step meetings regularly talked differently and all my senses were alert trying to grasp every word.

It was decided by a group conscience vote to hold weekly Step meetings and monthly Tradition meetings. The Tradition meetings became a challenge for me. I was so enthusiastic to do something, to get to know this program better, that I offered to translate one Tradition every month.

I became eager to learn more and said yes to all service—committees, national service, volunteer work at the GSO. It was in service that I started to like myself. A lot of my good qualities came alive, stronger than ever. I also learned to listen to others and respect their opinions. The program itself became my Higher Power and I gained complete trust in it and still have that trust today.

I still hadn't learned to apply this wonderful program at home. For the first time in my life I faced myself—the intolerant, inconsiderate, judgmental, controlling, angry person I was.

For the first time in my life I went on my knees and asked for help.

My husband and I started talking again but a few weeks later he reacted the way he had always done. I reacted in my usual way—"that selfish, no-good, irresponsible creature will never change." I poured this out to an Al-Anon friend and she asked me quietly why I was so angry.

For the first time in years the word love came to my mind. I still loved that "no-good, unchangeable, irresponsible" man. I cried because of things I had said and done to hurt this human being whose only crime was to get sick and love me at the same time.

Recovery took a long time and was often painful. It's not always easy to take life on life's terms, but there is progress in our marriage today.

Iceland

What spiritual gifts have I received from service?

Letting Go

I came to Al-Anon with a lot of problems, but I didn't believe at all in a God or a Higher Power. The Steps were very difficult to understand because of the language problem, but what I really got a grip on were the slogans.

I didn't like the slogan "Let Go and Let God," but after hearing a woman sharing her experience with the slogan I thought, "I'll try to use the first part of the slogan—Let Go."

I wrapped the problem and threw it over my shoulder with the movement of throwing; that was, for me, letting go. There were things that got solved after I had thrown them over my shoulder, so I started thinking, "Is there really a God that solved that problem?"

The more I did it, the more I started to believe there was a Higher Power. I began to feel grateful and to thank something or someone I couldn't see. After a few months, I could say the whole slogan and feel very comfortable with it.

Then years later, problems arose again and I lost my trust in this simple way. I thought, "I want to find out what a Higher Power really is." I asked many people to explain what their Higher Power looked like, who it was, where it was, etc. Nobody could give me a satisfying answer and I became very tense and frustrated.

I thought, "I'll take the sun as my Higher Power," but when I felt sad I didn't look at the sun, so it didn't help.

Then I thought, "I'll take the grass as my Higher Power, because when I feel down I look down." In those moments I didn't think of a Higher Power, so that didn't solve my problem.

After trying a few different things, I had to come to the conclusion that I had to go back to Keep It Simple and use the slogan Let Go and Let God again, because that worked. Without knowing what it is, where it is, who it is, I know that it's there when I ask for help and let go.

Belgium

Can I recall a time when letting go of a problem solved it?

The Program Is My Higher Power

When I was a child, my thoughts of God were benevolent. Not until I went to a religious boarding school was I persuaded that God was to be feared. This attitude continued for many years. Coming into Al-Anon, I heard about a Higher Power (was this God?), and I felt greatly confused.

To have faith in anything, for me, began with my group, then sharing with my sponsor, reading the literature, and working the program the best I could.

Meditating made me start to feel this "Power greater than ourselves." When I say feel, I mean I had more confidence, my fears diminished, and I could show love. My attitudes were changing thanks to the God of my understanding.

Praying, for me, is a nightly ritual, though I do keep in touch during the day sometimes mainly to show my gratitude.

My spirituality is the Al-Anon spirit that works within me. Alcohol is not affecting me today, but life is. If I use the tools available, I have a spiritual discipline that allows me to cope with, and also enjoy, whatever happens, One Day at a Time.

England

Where do I feel a Higher Power working in my program today?

Sponsorship

A common aspect of Al-Anon in which I feel the guidance of a Higher Power is sponsorship. Of course my sponsor makes no claim to be God or even to have a special relationship with any version of a higher, greater, or wiser authority, but I find in our talks a sense of reassurance and guidance that often feels miraculous. In general, the sign that something special has been given to me is the point in our conversation when I start to laugh at my problems.

When I find myself unexpectedly joking about the troubles that have been weighing me down, I know my burden has been lessened and that I have received a gift of healing from beyond myself.

United States

What spiritual guidance have I received from my sponsor?

Service Thank-You

The greatest thing my Higher Power arranged for me recently was to bring me into service for Al-Anon at an international level. I can't express how important this was for my understanding of Al-Anon and its program. To see and to feel that Al-Anon is really "worldwide," knowing I can attend Al-Anon meetings all over the world in order to feel at home in any part of the world, is a very special spiritual gift for me. By knowing and feeling the international base of our community, I have a deeper and more fundamental understanding of Al-Anon.

It is still difficult for me to have contact with my Higher Power and to meditate or to take my daily inventory, but I realize that it works, One Day at a Time. Once there came a day I could very easily say, "Please restore me to sanity and please let me know your will for me." And I know that there will be more spiritual awakenings waiting to happen in my life. I am looking forward to them.

Germany

How has my Higher Power provided me
direction in service?

Practicing These Principles

My conscious contact with God as I understand Him has been a continuous practice since I arrived in Al-Anon about fifteen years ago.

I was coming from a relationship that was deteriorating but there still was a willingness to go on together. Faith and confidence were so little in my day-by-day living and I had invited the God of my understanding to go away.

When my spouse found an AA room, his acceptance of alcoholism as a disease and his willingness to try the Twelve Steps to help himself brought relief for my pain. However, this resentful, hurt, and suspicious person stayed within me and it didn't allow my inner growth.

I was able to find the Al-Anon program a few months after his sobriety and it gave me a great discovery: now I can speak freely the things I cannot tell my husband. This sense of relief has encouraged me to get involved with Al-Anon services, read Al-Anon Conference Approved Literature and attend meetings.

I have tried, along these years, to apply this program in my life "in all my affairs." I have another alcoholic loved one, one of my four children. Since this realization I have gone through several difficult circumstances but fortunately, this time with my sober husband's support.

My spiritual awakening has not come suddenly, surprisingly, in an instantaneous light form. It has been achieved One Day at a Time in several ways.

Some examples are turning my son's life and will over to God, even when everything around seemed the opposite; understanding my group's fellows and accepting them as they are, even though my inner impulses do not help; accepting unfavorable and unexpected news and situations with my other children while my old attitudes are overwhelming my head; facing the challenges of Al-Anon service when everything around seems unfavorable.

Among all these conditions, my faith in a Higher Power has been the channel through which I have risen above every difficulty, and have made good use of them as opportunities to grow.

My experience with spirituality has often shown me that living with and understanding pain can bring spiritual growth, just as appreciating little daily joys can strengthen faith.

The more I feel my smallness and powerlessness, the more I grow in spirituality.

Portugal

What trials have I used as opportunities to grow?

My Service Thank-You

I want to share with you, my dear friends, my service work. When I came to Al-Anon I was unhappy and I didn't see what other people did for me. Today I want to thank all Al-Anons for saving my life, because my life will never be the same as before I came to Al-Anon.

Today my "thank-you" and gratitude is service in Al-Anon. Fourteen group representatives and I participate in the work meetings. We discuss using the Twelve Traditions to provide information about Al-Anon in my town and local area, to better help other suffering people. I have been chosen as a representative from this group. I take part in Al-Anon service meetings all over Poland. My task is to translate Al-Anon literature. My English is simple, but the language of the heart is simple as well. I learn service, structure, and love together in Al-Anon.

Poland

Have I found spirituality through service?

Chapter 8

Gratitude Leads to Growth

Al-Anon's international spirituality is summarized in one word: gratitude. Members take care to give thanks for the benefits of the Al-Anon program by recognizing the miracles they have seen in themselves and others.

Gratitude can take many forms, from a simple moment's prayer to a detailed inventory. It also includes many actions that arise from the desire to share one's gifts with others. It is said in Al-Anon that, gratitude reaches forward. There exists no more fulfilling way of giving thanks for gifts received than passing those same gifts on to others.

Now I Am Happy

First of all, I want to thank my Higher Power for having given me the gift to live with an alcoholic and the opportunity to have arrived at an Al-Anon room.

I got married very early to a good man without any bad habits and we had two sons. When the first one was one year and six months old and the second one was only eight months old, my husband died. I suffered so much but kept my faith in God.

Later I met another man; he had no chance to give me a good material life but he gave me some things I always looked for in a human being: kindness, honor, and a rich spiritual life, even though he was a problem drinker.

We have been together for ten years. We have a daughter and a son and my husband took on with love my first two sons. My life was like a black cavern. Everything was messed up. After so much fighting, shame, and my trying to get him to stop drinking, at last he arrived at an AA room. Now he is sober for three years. At that time he took me to Al-Anon so I could find out alcoholism is a disease. At first it was hard for me to accept that, it sounded like nonsense, but when I read the Twelve Steps, there was the First Step saying "...we were powerless over alcohol—that our lives had become unmanageable."

I thought and thought about that and really I could understand we cannot change anyone. I was surprised to hear from my fellows in the Al-Anon meetings that such fellowship is not religious, but spiritual.

Al-Anon has helped me to know myself. I am 35 years old and now I am happy. I have found my inner light, my Higher Power. I feel at peace and want to thank Al-Anon to let me know such a simple program, sharing experience, love, faith, strength and hope with the fellows. Today I have faith in myself and I am recovering "Step by Step." I can hear what I like and dislike without getting hurt and I can share without expectation of controlling anyone. I have learned a new way of living and the wisdom to accept myself as I am. Now any hindrance I face is a stepping stone to my growth.

I practice the program, I read the literature, and I still have so much to learn. I don't want to be perfect; all I want is to keep on with the program and enjoy this new way of life.

Thank you, Al-Anon fellowship as a whole.

Brazil

How has self-acceptance helped me to enjoy my life?

An Alphabet of Gratitude

If I can't sleep at night, I often use the time when I would otherwise be tossing and turning to pray. Especially if I have a problem that's troubling me, I sometimes try composing a gratitude list starting with A and going as far toward Z as I can progress before I fall asleep. I first read about this practice in *As We Understood...*, shortly after hearing it described in meetings. Over the years it has served me well.

Often I'll detour at a particular letter and find myself giving thanks for apples and alexandrites, apothecaries and astronauts, ants and anchovies, or bottles and bakeries, bumblebees and blueberries, bathtubs and brushes.

The more overwhelming the problem I'm entertaining, the more my gratitude list helps me. First, by taking my mind off of my obsession, and second, by reminding me of the multitude of delightful and peculiar items in the world around me. I move from my troubled personal perspective toward what I imagine to be the perspective of my Higher Power, from which my pain is a small part of a larger landscape that is filled with endless possibilities.

As I work on my list with increasing wonder, I feel more deeply the healing influence of my Higher Power in every area of my life.

United States

What would I include in my alphabet of gratitude?

Another Way

Before Al-Anon, I once heard a speaker describe most people as standing atop the wreckage of their lives, proudly proclaiming, "I did it my way."

I can't speak for most people, but I know I felt that the essence of my life had been captured in that description. My life was an example of destructive self-will but I didn't know how else to live.

In Al-Anon I have discovered another way, one in which a Power greater than myself seems to provide guidance. Part of the profound difference I see in the way I live is that I trust this power, even though I cannot define, isolate, taste, touch or see it.

In a way for which I feel little understanding but truly profound gratitude, I am given a sense of peace and fulfillment beyond what I have ever known. This is my version of spiritual experience: I can't quite tell you what brought me here, but I can say with certainty that the journey has been worth the effort.

United States

***Do I see evidence in my life of spiritual
benefits that I cannot explain?***

Gratitude

A few years ago on a quiet Saturday morning I got a phone call from a friend who told me his older brother had suddenly died. That day was one of the saddest of my life. I was close to the whole family, and both brothers had been among my best friends since child-hood.

After the initial shock of grief, I found myself going through the day deliberately giv-ing thanks for every aspect of my life that came to mind. I thanked my Higher Power for the long friendship I had enjoyed as well as every incident of joy, challenge, discovery, and appreciation. I even gave thanks for my own grief at the loss of such a loyal friend.

Then I began an even more deliberate exercise in gratitude in which I just took con-scious notice of all that was still good in my life: family, friends, sunshine, health, music, flowers, birds, even the simple sensation of just drawing breath. I realized that my life was still filled with miracles and that, while I didn't know why my friend had died so young, I definitely knew that part of the reason he had lived was to give me the gift of a deep and lasting friendship.

In practicing gratitude I realized I still felt sustained by a Higher Power and that, while my friend had died, the love on which our friendship rested was still very much alive.

United States

When does gratitude in Al-Anon help me feel a connection to the God of my understanding?

Thanks to My Higher Power

Thanks to my Higher Power, the God of my understanding, for guiding me into this beautiful fellowship. I feel nothing happens by accident; everything is planned by God. If my husband were not an alcoholic, I would not have become an Al-Anon member. God does things for the good of those He loves. I am very grateful to the local members of Al-Anon who are really God-sent people. I also feel very happy to say the first Al-Anon member that I met is my sponsor who writes me regularly.

Ever since I heard alcoholism is a disease I started changing my attitude toward the alcoholic. I became aware of my shortcomings and all the insane things I had done— neglecting my appearance, home, children, school work, etc.—because apart from my husband I was affected by the drinking of my father, brother, brother-in-law, cousins and friends. When I started attending Al-Anon meetings, which gave me great courage and strength, I learned a lot from this simple program. It has made me a better person, but I must say not overnight— rather on a One Day at a Time basis.

I must admit my powerlessness over alcohol and that life is unmanageable. I tried everything but nothing worked. While I was attending Al-Anon meetings, my husband made up his mind to join a rehabilitation center for four months. He slipped on two occasions but he could not drink in peace, and he got sober again.

We spent a very happy Silver Anniversary together. We went for a honeymoon to a sea resort and made up for lost time, making amends. After we celebrated our anniversary, my husband kept getting a pain in his throat. We went to the doctor. It was a growth on one of the vocal cords. My husband died a year later, sober, of cancer of the throat, another killer disease. It was a beautiful funeral. I received much love from the AA, Al-Anon, and Alateen members of my area. I accepted my husband's death calmly and many people were astonished to see the change in me. Meetings and reading of the Twelve Steps and Traditions are a part of my life now, though at the earlier stage I used to miss meetings and make a lot of excuses, taking in only sharings that interested me.

A wonderful thing about Al-Anon is that I was encouraged to renew my faith in a Power greater than myself. I thought I was beaten. I forgot that God gave me the strength and the means to live. I learned to identify with the Divine Principle that rules my life. This is a spiritual program and ever reminds me that God is by my side.

India

*How do I express my gratitude for the
guidance I have received in Al-Anon?*

Conclusion

The principles of the Al-Anon program foster a rich variety of spiritual responses in many different languages and cultures. As we strive to practice Al-Anon's spiritual program in our daily lives, we can take heart from reflecting that the exact same principles are working miracles in the lives of other members around the world. A "Power greater than ourselves" is helping us find solutions to the problem of living with the effects of alcoholism, no matter what our backgrounds or beliefs. No matter what our differences, we share our experiences of the healing power within the spiritual principles of the Al-Anon program.

Since alcoholism fails to recognize barriers of race, religion, culture, or nationality, the members of Al-Anon are splendidly diverse. Our fellowship reaches out with a common purpose to over one hundred countries around the world.

As Al-Anon's suggested closing puts it, "May the understanding, love and peace of the program grow in you One Day at a Time." May you be open to the spiritual ideas found in this book and to those of others as we continue to join hands in the circle of love and caring that is Al-Anon.

Al-Anon's Declaration

Let It Begin With Me
When anyone, anywhere, reaches out for help
let the hand of Al-Anon and Alateen
always be there, and — Let It Begin With Me.

The Working Principles of Al-Anon

The basic ideas of Al-Anon, like those of Alcoholics Anonymous, are as old as recorded history. They are the concepts on which all spiritual philosophies are based. These elements are:

Acknowledgment of our dependence on a Supreme Being.

Love for our fellow man and recognition of his dignity and value. Awareness of the need to improve ourselves through self-appraisal and admitting to our faults.

Belief in the effective spiritual power of true personal humility and conscious gratitude. Willingness to help others.

The working philosophy of Al-Anon is a pattern for right living, for overcoming difficulties and for helping us to achieve our aspirations.

We come into Al-Anon to solve the specific problem of alcoholism and its disastrous effect on our lives. We apply the basic spiritual ideas by means of what we call the Twelve Steps. These are reinforced by the Twelve Traditions, by the Serenity Prayer and by a group of concepts known simply as the Slogans.

It All Begins with Words

The mere words which make up the Steps, the Traditions, the Serenity Prayer and the Slogans may be read by anybody in a manner of minutes. It takes much more than a superficial reading, however, to produce understanding and results. The ideas contained in the words, applied to our daily lives, can bring about unimaginable changes for the better, but only to the degree that we absorb and use them.

They provide a key to spiritual enlightenment that has an almost miraculous effect on human affairs by changing our thinking and our attitudes in relation to others. They can, and do, release people from problems brought about by compulsive drinking. But we ourselves must do the work that brings these changes about.

first published in *Al-Anon Faces Alcoholism* p.229

Having Had a Spiritual Awakening…

THE TWELVE STEPS

1. We admitted we were powerless over alcohol—that our lives had become unmanageable.
2. Came to believe that a Power greater than ourselves could restore us to sanity.
3. Made a decision to turn our will and our lives over to the care of God *as we understood Him*.
4. Made a searching and fearless moral inventory of ourselves.
5. Admitted to God, to ourselves and to another human being the exact nature of our wrongs.
6. Were entirely ready to have God remove all these defects of character.
7. Humbly asked Him to remove our shortcomings.
8. Made a list of all persons we had harmed, and became willing to make amends to them all.
9. Made direct amends to such people wherever possible, except when to do so would injure them or others.
10. Continued to take personal inventory and when we were wrong promptly admitted it
11. Sought through prayer and meditation to improve our conscious contact with God *as we understood Him*, praying only for knowledge of His will for us and the power to carry that out.
12. Having had a spiritual awakening as the result of these Steps, we tried to carry this message to others, and to practice these principles in all our affairs.

THE TWELVE TRADITIONS

1. Our common welfare should come first; personal progress for the greatest number depends upon unity.
2. For our group purpose there is but one authority—a loving God as He may express Himself in our group conscience. Our leaders are but trusted servants; they do not govern.
3. The relatives of alcoholics, when gathered together for mutual aid, may call them selves an Al-Anon Family Group, provided that, as a group, they have no other affiliation. The only requirement for membership is that there be a problem of alcoholism in a relative or friend.
4. Each group should be autonomous, except in matters affecting another group or Al-Anon or AA as a whole.
5. Each Al-Anon Family Group has but one purpose: to help families of alcoholics. We do this by practicing the Twelve Steps of AA *ourselves*, by encouraging and understanding our alcoholic relatives, and by welcoming and giving comfort to families of alcoholics.
6. Our Al-Anon Family Groups ought never endorse, finance or lend our name to any outside enterprise, lest problems of money, property and prestige divert us from our primary spiritual aim. Although a separate entity, we should always cooperate with Alcoholics Anonymous.
7. Every group ought to be fully self-supporting, declining outside contributions.
8. Al-Anon Twelfth-Step work should remain forever non-professional, but our service centers may employ special workers.
9. Our groups, as such, ought never be organized; but we may create service boards or committees directly responsible to those they serve.
10. The Al-Anon Family Groups have no opinion on outside issues; hence our name ought never be drawn into public controversy.
11. Our public relations policy is based on attraction rather than promotion; we need always maintain personal anonymity at the level of press, radio, TV and films. We need guard with special care the anonymity of all AA members.
12. Anonymity is the spiritual foundation of all our Traditions, ever reminding us to place principles above personalities.

Having Had a Spiritual Awakening…

THE TWELVE CONCEPTS OF SERVICE

1. The ultimate responsibility and authority for Al-Anon world services belongs to the Al-Anon groups.
2. The Al-Anon Family Groups have delegated complete administrative and operational authority to their Conference and its service arms.
3. The Right of Decision makes effective leadership possible.
4. Participation is the key to harmony.
5. The Rights of Appeal and Petition protect minorities and assure that they be heard.
6. The Conference acknowledges the primary administrative responsibility of the trustees.
7. The trustees have legal rights while the rights of the Conference are traditional.
8. The Board of Trustees delegates full authority for routine management of the Al-Anon Headquarters to its executive committees.
9. Good personal leadership at all service levels is a necessity. In the field of world service the Board of Trustees assumes the primary leadership.
10. Service responsibility is balanced by carefully defined service authority and double-headed management is avoided.
11. The World Service Office is composed of standing committees, executives and staff members.
12. The spiritual foundation for Al-Anon's world service is contained in the General Warranties of the Conference, Article 12 of the Charter.

GENERAL WARRANTIES

In all its proceedings the World Service Conference of Al-Anon shall observe the spirit of the Traditions:

1. that only sufficient operating funds, including an ample reserve, be its prudent financial principle;
2. that no Conference member shall be placed in unqualified authority over other members;
3. that all decisions be reached by discussion, vote and, whenever possible, by unanimity;
4. that no Conference action ever be personally punitive or an incitement to public controversy;
5. that though the Conference serves Al-Anon, it shall never perform any act of government; and that, like the fellowship of Al-Anon Family Groups which it serves, it shall always remain democratic in thought and action.

Appreciation goes to...

...the 1994 World Service Conference members who approved the creation of this book with the following motion: "To produce a recovery piece on spirituality affirming the universality of our fellowship from the perspective of a variety of cultures around the world."

...the many Al-Anon/Alateen members worldwide who submitted stories, photos and artwork.

...the writer, editors, designers and reviewers who applied their many talents to this labor of love.

...all those who serve families and friends of alcoholics worldwide.

...our diverse understanding of spirituality.

Index

Note: The words God, God of my understanding, Higher Power, and Spirituality are used throughout this book and are not included in the index.

Having Had a Spiritual Awakening...

— My Spiritual Reflections —

— My Spiritual Reflections —

— My Spiritual Reflections —

— My Spiritual Reflections —

— My Spiritual Reflections —

— My Spiritual Reflections —

– My Spiritual Reflections –